A SHORT GUIDE TO

ISLAM

ELIZABETH
PELTOLA

A
SHORT
GUIDE
TO

ISLAM

A Biblical Response
to the Faith of Our
MUSLIM NEIGHBORS

PUBLISHING
BRENTWOOD, TENNESSEE

To Mr. Fleming, for empowering a motley crew of college students to live for Jesus and love "every tribe and nation"

But as for you, continue in what you have learned and have become convinced of, because you know those from whom you learned it, and how from infancy you have know the Holy Scriptures, which are able to make you wise for salvation through faith in Christ Jesus. All Scripture is God-breathed and is useful for teaching, rebuking, correcting and training in righteousness, so that the servant of God may be thoroughly equipped for every good work. (2 Tim. 3:14–17 NKJV)

Acknowledgments

THANK YOU DEAR PEKKA, your unwavering support means the world. As a husband you empower where others suppress, protect and lead our home, and keep us grounded on Jesus. Your love points me to God's love.

My heart is full when I think of my team at One Truth Project (www.onetruthproject.org), Mansah and Ellen, where friendship and happiness meet each week as we work together on resources for the church. Thank you for the "writing days."

Ongoing gratitude to the Blackham family, whose love for Jesus, their immense knowledge of Church history, and deep grasp of the holy Trinity help my family go deep into the knowledge of God, empowering our conversations with Muslims.

Deep thanks to our little church who carve out space each Sunday to ponder the love and sacrifice of God for us. Gratitude for your prayers faithfully lifting us up to our heavenly Father, and buying each new book as they are released! That in itself is a blessing.

My parents, Papa the printer, who understands publishing inside and out, and Mum whose grasp of grammar is like none other. Thank you for reading my work, pointing out different theologies and giving me food for thought.

Thankful for the gifted team who have brought this book to light. Their editing expertise and guidance has made this journey a joy. Mary, your positive and helpful interactions are a gift to writers.

This book travels through decades of life lived with fellow Christians among Muslim communities. Mission friends like Marta, Val, and Swabie are hard to come by. I treasure our many adventures, some of which are in this book. Each story helped deepen our understanding of Islam and Muslim cultures.

Love and thanks to my Muslim friends. We may not agree on who God is, but your friendship is precious, and our conversations thought-provoking. I still long for you to know Jesus as God and Savior, to share eternal life together, that will always be my prayer, but for now I treasure the friendship, laughter and of course, discussions!

At twenty-two years of age I started working with a cross-cultural interdenominational team, building a church among Kurdish refugees in London. Those four formative years learning Turkish, serving alongside Roger, Yvonne, Joy, Brian, and the team, some of whom were exiled from Islamic lands for successful Christian witness, laid a solid foundation for biblical engagement of Islam, while also gifting me with some of the dearest friends.

Tu Vero Permane, But Continue Thou
Primary School motto, Central Africa.

Contents

Part 3: Understanding Islamic Differences

Part 4: Understanding Migration and Mission

Part 5: Understanding Theological Differences

Held Back

Sitting on the floor of a refugee's home in a London council flat, eating delicious Central Asian food, I sat, eager to share what I knew of Christ with my new Muslim friends, yet I remained silent.

The TV blared out Turkish cultural debates, then Kurdish folk music, culminating with disturbing, depressing, and slightly scary Islamic stories of revenge. A fascinating part of living life with those who belong to another culture and religion. Conversations started soon became stunted as a consequence of adhering to Islamic cultural norms over gospel opportunities.

At twenty-two-years-old, I clearly saw something was wrong with how stifled I felt, unable to share a message of hope in a home that needed to know the love of Jesus. What had led to my inability to communicate the only way to everlasting help and hope?!

Two things hindered me that day—mission manuals emphasizing how to avoid cultural faux pas and, perhaps the greater issue, my own fear! Together they quashed the freedom of spontaneous gospel witness. Forgotten was a new Christian worker's true authority—one from heaven!

THE CONTENT OF THOSE mission manuals, found a few years earlier in Christian college libraries, had given long lists of what to do and what not to do when moving among Muslim communities. They suggested Christians wait for full assimilation into a culture and acceptance by its people to speak about Christ and then only after you've earned respect from Muslims. They emphasized obedience to cultural suppressions and encouraged women never to speak to a man. These instructions left me, a new missionary, in a quandary, especially when the fathers of the homes I was visiting asked me about the Turkish-speaking church I attended.

Then there was the occasion when an older brother of a teen-age girl who had joined our church was interested in joining our bilingual youth group. Meanwhile, the mother wanted to read the dregs of my small coffee cup (fortune-telling), and extended family members and friends from the same community began asking about spiritual matters. Rather than happily pour out the wonders of Jesus and all that He has done for us, I stumbled and ummed and aahed, and ultimately I completely failed to share the gospel.

BIBLICALLY RESPONDING TO ISLAM

Those manuals were not helpful for the Western context I was serving in, and they didn't seem to help when living in bustling cities in Islamic lands. I had to discover how to be a clear gospel witness within these different contexts.

Compromise had stemmed from emphasizing religious behaviors and cultural norms rather than responding with confidence to the prompting of the Lord: a prompting to speak, to proclaim His name among those who don't believe.

If the Lord tells us He will give us the words to speak when hauled before antagonistic courts (Luke 12:11–12), then surely He can break through any cultural religious norms to empower inexperienced twenty-two-year-old missionaries to speak courageously for Him, especially when we are speaking with a refugee family who has newly arrived in the Western world. Yes. He can. He can also cut through our fears and empower us to serve in any circumstance and community.

Throughout history, biblically literate Christians have responded to Islam, and the last twenty years have seen more good books filled with wise advice for those who wish to engage the religion of Islam and the people who adhere to it. And right here we start with a helpful distinction: how we engage the religion of Islam may differ from how we engage its people.

So, why another book on the subject? Big gaps exist in the resources available to Christians who wish to *biblically* understand Islam. Many secular commentators offer opinions on Islam. Those opinions rose to the forefront after America and Europe experienced horrendous attacks, when some radical followers of Islam wounded many within our shores.

Yet one group of people can understand Islam better than any secular commentator. Only one group can respond with religious insight into the world of Islam, and that is the Christian world. Some might say this sounds arrogant—who are Christians to say they have the monopoly on understanding Islam? True, no one can completely understand a religion that is not their own. Many Christians are often misunderstood when outsiders misjudge the central Person of Christianity and our relationship with Him, but *He* is why Christians can confidently engage the world of Islam. He is why we can offer a solution to the terrors on the world stage connected with Islamic law and the example of Muhammad seen implemented within our societies. We build our lives on "the truth" (John 8:31–32; John 14:6), which means we can recognize when something is a counterfeit. Just like those who identify counterfeit money, Christians know what is false because they have studied the real thing.

We build our lives on "the truth" (John
8:31–32; John 14:6), which means we can
recognize when something is a counterfeit.

As we enter the world of understanding Islam, it is helpful
to question some current myths circulating throughout society.
These myths are not only found in Christian environments but
also propagated by secular commentators, repeated by journalists,
professors, and Christian ministers alike. They are far-reaching
myths, and adopting them can have far-reaching consequences.

As we question those modern myths and trends, let's start
by asking what the Bible says about them. Once we tackle the
myths, we'll compare Islamic theology with biblical theology.
We'll also consider how religious people engage with their own
texts and how we understand what a religion teaches.

Muslims propagate the same myths to advance Islam.
Secularists do likewise, often simplifying religions by putting
them into manageable categories, but this prevents them from
understanding the intricacies of different faith traditions.

For Christians who follow suit, perhaps their misperception
comes from thinking that *sameness* means "agreement" or that
being similar is the path to unity. This is far from the truth.
It is a biblical position to categorically disagree with someone,

including those who hate us, and genuinely love them at the same time. Why? How? Not through any power of our own but through the power of the Holy Spirit.

God shows this in that while we were still enemies, He died for us (Rom. 5:8–10). Talk about loving those you disagree with?!

Does Islam have such a life-changing example in its version of god?

We need to biblically examine the claims made by Christians and non-Christians alike. We need to be sure we aren't starting our investigation into one of the world's fastest growing religions with falsehood. We can't address every claim, but we'll begin our nosedive into biblically understanding Islam by responding to five popular misconceptions.

These mistruths address both theological and evangelistic responses to Islam and Muslims. We'll engage the world of Islam both in theory and with practical application, starting with some of the most hazardous modern myths:

1. People just need to believe in God.
2. Christianity and Islam are the same, or similar.
3. Islam is Abrahamic.
4. Start with Islam in evangelism among Muslims.

5. Stay away from Jesus, the Trinity, and the Old Testament when you witness to Muslims.

DISCUSS AND REFLECT

1. Who can respond with religious insight into the Islamic world?

2. Why can Christians categorically disagree with people yet love them?

3. What bad advice can hold Christians back in their witness among Muslims?

4. Who is the reason for Christians' ability to understand Islam?

5. What are five myths we need to engage with and provide a biblical response to?

PART 1

Challenging Modern Myths

CHAPTER 1

Myth One: People Just Need to Believe in God

In the Midwest, at a beautiful college near the Mississippi River, young adults and older teens lifted their voices in song and prayer during daily chapel service. Their instruments and voices were symphonic, their dedication admirable, and their prayers earnest. Yet something struck a chord of disquiet deep down. Every prayer was addressed to God. All closed their thoughts with, "in Jesus's name," a wonderful way to end a prayer, but no one addressed our heavenly Father personally. There was nothing wrong with their opening address: "Dear God," but something was missing.

AT THIS POINT IN life, many of those college students had not had much interaction with people of other faiths. They knew who they were talking to in their prayers. They knew the Father, the Son, and the Holy Spirit. Yet their address was also typical of many modern Christians. In our praises, thanksgivings, and pleas to God, we sometimes forget to specifically describe *who* we are praying to. He isn't only God. He is Father, which is how Jesus modeled prayer in Matthew 6. He is both transcendent and near, both authoritative over all and actively engaged in the everyday. We forget how exceptional our God truly is.

The trinitarian, holy God, seen throughout the Bible, is a profound challenge to every human idea about God. The essence of the Father, the Son, and the Holy Spirit challenges Islam at its core. The great command of Jesus, recorded in Matthew 28, to go and baptize "in the name of the Father, the Son, and the Holy Spirit" holds Islam to account. Why? Because the Qur'an, Islam's holy book, denies the Holy Trinity. Islam has no heavenly father, no eternal son, and no holy spirit indwelling its believers.

It isn't enough for us just to believe in a god. The god of Islam, Allah, has no relation to the triune God. A whole book could be written on this crucial doctrine, but keep reading as we'll go into some detail about Allah in the chapters ahead.

Much of the world believes in a god or gods. Secularists live according to their gods—health, materialism, intelligence, and more. Buddhists seek a higher plane of spirituality where our material being becomes nothing. Hindus adhere to gods and hope for assimilation into the highest of gods. Pagans worship elements and gods, seeking peace through spirituality and meditations. All people have gods of some sort or another. These are the same kinds of gods the Bible repeatedly warns us about (Job 31:24–28; 2 Kings 23:5–11; Isa. 44; Matt. 6:24), proclaiming they cannot hear or act on behalf of those who cry out to them. The foreign gods of the nations around God's people would not help them but would pull them away from the true God who was with them. Today, Christians serve this one true God who moves and acts to rescue us from evil. This is the God who saves.

As we engage with Islamic beliefs about our God, we pray trustingly to our heavenly Father for insight because my heart, and I pray your heart, is that Muslims, whom God loves would know and love Him as the one true God. All roads *do not* lead to the God of the Bible, and all religions *do not* serve the same God, just with different names. As a stark contrast to other gods, we worship the Lord Jesus who suffered for us through His agonizing death. We then think on His spectacular resurrection and rejoice as we consider His ascension to His throne. We know the Holy Spirit lives in us and helps us commune with the Son and the Father. This God we must seek to share in our conversations with Muslims. The God of the Bible is not ambiguous or unknowable; no, that is Allah. Rather, God the Father and His Son are with us through the work of the Holy Spirit (John 14:16–20; Rom. 8:11). Keep this God at the core of conversations with Muslims, and worthwhile discussions will emerge.

As we engage with Islamic beliefs
about our God, we pray trustingly to
our heavenly Father for insight because
my heart, and I pray your heart, is that
Muslims, whom God loves would know
and love Him as the one true God.

DISCUSS AND REFLECT

1. How does the biblical God contrast with other gods?

2. Is it okay just to believe in God? Why or why not?

3. What Bible verses speak about other gods, and what does the Bible say about them?

4. Why does the Great Commission hold Islam to account?

5. Whom do we keep at the heart of our conversations with Muslims?

CHAPTER 2

Myth Two: Islam and Christianity Are Similar

"Why are you two debating each other? Don't you believe the same thing?" A bemused atheist stood by listening to a Muslim ask questions about the Christian faith. He didn't like either religion but began to challenge me, pointing to a "historically violent Christianity," a "violent Bible," while ignoring the glaring examples found throughout the Qur'an. Initially antagonistic and mocking, loud and accusing, his questions were good ones—misinformed but good. "Those are great questions that I'd like to think about a bit more, but here's an initial response. . . ." After hearing an affirmation of his questions, his whole demeanor changed, and there began a positive interaction between people whose views of the world stood poles apart.

In future scenarios, when hounded by Muslim antagonists, the atheist became strangely supportive of me. He began to acknowledge many good elements of Christianity and how different it was to Islam. He even acknowledged Christianity's influence in promoting peace-filled societies!

YOU MAY HAVE HEARD the widespread opinion that religions are all the same, including that they are to blame for violence in the world, narrow thinking, and lack of freedoms. Exposed scandals of abuse and unfaithfulness among church clergy do nothing to dispel this opinion. These scandals do not sum up the whole of the church, and to think they do would be an inaccurate way of looking at Christianity.[1] Nor is it right to categorize the church as narrow and freedom suppressors; on the contrary Jesus and biblical attitudes make us free (John 8:36; Gal. 5:22–23). Though not as the world sees it. Traditional Islam certainly sees Christianity and secularism as immoral, needing the boundaries and laws offered by Islamic law.

Modern society seems to enjoy assigning people to narrow categories. It seems more manageable to belittle God's creative, diverse, and wonderfully complex world into convenient subgroups. This work of sorting into the lowest common denominator is how religions are often misunderstood. We will spend time considering the differences between the God of the Bible and Allah throughout the book, especially in part 5, but the differences reach much farther. If the message of Islam and Christianity are the same, then Muslims and Christians must be confused. Let's unpack this point further, by looking at three key areas of biblical truth: (1) the Lord Jesus, (2) His death on a cross, and (3) the Holy Trinity.

THREE KEY AREAS OF BIBLICAL TRUTH

1. Islam has no Jesus.

Islam has a remarkable fellow called Isa. In Islamic texts we read of Isa's many miracles, which are like the miracles of Jesus, but unlike Jesus, he is preoccupied with denying his divinity (Q 4:171, 5:17, 72–78, 116; 43:64). He is also a created being (Q 3:45 47). The Messiah, Jesus, the son of Mary, was but a messenger of Allah, and His word which He directed to Mary and a soul (created at a command) from Him. So believe in Allah and His messengers (Q 4:171).[2] The Qur'an says that this fellow Isa, whom Muslims believe is Jesus, did not die. Contrast this to the biblical and historical Jesus, who is coeternal with the Father, with Him in the beginning (John 1:1). His death on the cross made a way for us to be made right with God. Death was the necessary payment, and Jesus paid it for us. The Qur'an categorically makes this impossible: "no bearer of burdens will bear the burden of another" (Q 6:164; 35:18).

2. There is no crucifixion in Islam.

"And [for] their saying, 'Indeed, we have killed the Messiah, Jesus, the son of Mary, the messenger of Allah.' And they did not kill him, nor did they crucify him; but [another] was made to resemble him to them. And indeed, those who differ over it are in doubt about it. They have no knowledge of it except the following of assumption. And they did not kill him, for certain" (Q 4:157). It is incomprehensible to Muslims that God would die; the thought overwhelms most Christians with wonder and thanksgiving. Jesus's crucifixion brings us hope. He is the Suffering Servant (Isa. 53) who made a way for us to be made right and who understands our trials because He took on flesh (John 1:14) and lived among us. In Islam, Allah would not walk or speak with us, and he certainly could not die for us. We will go into much more detail in our chapter on God, in part 5.

3. There is no Trinity in Islam.

"Say, 'He is Allah, [who is] One, Allah, the Eternal Refuge. He neither begets nor is born, Nor is there to Him any equivalent'" (Q 112:1–4). When a Muslim friend says we believe in the same God, it's helpful to question them about the God we know: "So you believe in our heavenly Father, His Son Jesus, and the Holy Spirit?" The emphatic response will be *no*! Islam's god, referred to in Arabic as "the god" (Allah), is described as "one" (Tawhid). Allah is no Trinity. *Tawhid* is a core theological concept in Islam; it refers to the oneness of God. Not to be confused with the biblical idea that the Lord is one (Deut. 6:4; Mark 12:29), which we affirm alongside God's tri-unity. He is both one God and three Persons. The word *tawhid* is not mentioned in the Arabic Qur'an, but the idea is alluded to throughout Islamic theological writing. Allah is a singular being, and the Qur'an is concerned about explaining that Allah is not three and has no son (Q 4:171).

IS GOD INCONSISTENT?

We've quickly looked at three areas of core Christian doctrine. All three show how different the two religions are. If we believe Islam and Christianity are the same, or similar, then we sign up to a confused mishmash of contradictory beliefs.

Let's apply that same conclusion to God, the originator of our faith. If both Christian and Islamic theologies are of the same origin, or similar in content, then God is inconsistent or erratic. This is a terrible thought to consider and insulting to the Christian mind, no less for the Islamic. Combining the two undermines the divinity of Jesus. It defies biblical revelation. It presents a way of life against a biblical lifestyle. It undermines the way of salvation.

Christianity and Islam do not have the same view of life, behavior, and revelation about *who* God is and *how* God acts. There is no similarity between the core beliefs of the Christian faith and Islam. In this book we will draw a clear picture of the differences between the two, which will help us have a clear understanding of Islam.

DISCUSS AND REFLECT

1. Why do people today assign people to narrow categories?

2. What does Islam teach about Jesus?

3. What does Islam teach about His crucifixion?

4. What does Islam say about the Trinity?

5. If we believe Islam and Christianity are similar, what will the results be?

CHAPTER 3

Myth Three: Islam Is Abrahamic

Outside the beautiful exterior of the Houses of Parliament and Big Ben, next to Westminster Abbey in London, stood a vicar, a rabbi, and a Muslim cleric (an Imam). Sounds like a joke is forming, but unfortunately, the situation at hand had a serious side.

A terror attack had just occurred in London, just like in other parts of the world. Each time an attack lands on England's shores from its Islamic community, out comes the vicar, rabbi, an Imam, and often a politician. The Imam quotes, almost without fail, Qur'an 5:32, stating that "whoever kills a soul . . . it is as if he had slain mankind entirely. And whoever saves one—it is as if he had saved mankind entirely."

None of the journalists question their opinions, and the politician blindly agrees. Few bother to look up the verses being quoted.

ON ONE LEVEL WE all appreciate a scene of unity and concern shared by people who belong to different faiths, or nonfaith, groups. Yet the Imam's quote is worth further analysis. Their foundation of Abrahamic unity requires additional consideration if we are to biblically engage other religions.

Qur'an 5:32 begins with this statement "We decreed upon the Children of Israel that whoever kills a soul unless for a soul or for corruption . . . it is as if he had slain mankind." Note how the verse is addressed to Jews, within a chapter challenging Christian and Jewish theology and books. The verse has nothing to do with Muslims. The next verse, Qur'an 5:33, does address Muslims: "Indeed, the penalty for those who wage war against Allah and His Messenger and strive upon earth [to cause] corruption is none but that they be killed or crucified or that their hands and feet be cut off from opposite sides or that they be exiled from the land. That is for them a disgrace in this world; and for them in the Hereafter is a great punishment." The verses quoted by the vicar, rabbi, Imam, and politician do not teach an allegiance to the same God, the same books, or the same view of friend and foe. The behavior encouraged toward enemies of Islam undermines the teaching of Christ completely.

The idea of multiple Abrahamic religions is almost universally accepted in Western society. Yet it is a relatively new idea and originates in Islamic and secular thought, not in the Bible. Author Aaron Hughes sees its introduction into mainstream thought as a means to alleviate anti-Semitism during the twentieth century and encourage interfaith conversation: "We begin to witness the creation of an 'Abrahamic religions' discourse, one that encourages us to imagine something positive, a common faith of 'spiritual' bond that Jews, Christians and Muslims share in the present and are perceived to have had in the distant past."[1]

The idea entices Christians to see that Judaism and Christianity have a similar source and therefore are not at odds with each other. Its usage may have been entirely for practical reasons, to preserve unity and reduce racism, but it is gravely misguided, as it does not provide long-term solutions to abuse and racism. Yet this same principle has been applied to modern Christian missions among Muslims, using this as the foundation from which to build a conversation about Christ. What is the fallout from this?

ISLAMIZATION OF CHRISTIANITY

The eighteenth-century Enlightenment brought a pivot largely away from religion, including Christianity, toward secularism. Since then, we've generally struggled to provide a clear presentation of Jesus among Muslims in Islamic lands. A trend of combining religions (syncretism) emerged, influencing the removal of discussions on the Father, Son, and Holy Spirit from evangelistic conversations among Muslims and, dreadfully, even in some Bible translations for the Islamic world.

The perception of Islam and Christianity sharing its roots is taught in the Qur'an (Q 2:127–133), but it also works hard to undermine Abrahamic teaching, as we have seen in Qur'an 5:1–33, and introduces Abraham as a Muslim (Q 2:127–128). Just because a religion claims Abraham as one of their founders does not mean that he is.

Mark Durie, a Christian theologian and researcher on Christian-Muslim relations, also explores this important topic in his book *Which God?*. He outlines how in Islamic presentations to Christians, their doctrine that Allah is the God of the Bible is a central component. We need to be clear: this is an Islamic ideal, not Christian. It has been adopted by many modern Western Christians living outside of Islamic countries but is rarely adopted by Christians living inside Islamic lands unless they have been influenced by syncretistic Western missionaries or pressure from Islam.

In his excellent article titled "The Abrahamic Fallacy" he comments on the consequences of those who have upheld the theme of the three Abrahamic faiths as a way of unity between warring sides: "This vision of a political and spiritual reconciliation between faiths based upon a shared identity as followers of 'Abrahamic faith' is fundamentally flawed. In fact it leads to Islamization, as a society based on the Quranic concept of

Abrahamic faith is a sharia state, which by virtue of the structure of Islamic law, is devoted to the decline and ultimate disappearance of Christianity and Judaism."[2]

TRACING ROOTS

The key difference between the three main religions claiming roots in Abraham is how they view Jesus. Islam removes the historical Jesus from its core doctrines, which we'll tackle in more depth as we go through the book. Jesus has no place in modern-day Judaic teaching. Yet we see challenges to such beliefs throughout the Gospels (Matt. 26:63–68; 1 John 2:22–23).

Jesus Himself introduces His holy divine name to religious leaders who did not believe Him, when He states, "'Your father Abraham rejoiced to see my day; he saw it and was glad.' The Jews replied, 'You aren't fifty years old yet, and you've seen Abraham?' Jesus said to them, 'Truly I tell you, before Abraham was, I am'" (John 8:56–58; see a similar introduction in Exod. 3:14–15).

These are powerful verses to read with Muslim friends. They open up the truth of the Bible and challenge Qur'anic teaching about their Messiah, Isa (some of these teachings were mentioned earlier: Q 3:45; 4:157, 171–172; 9:30–31).

Let's stick with the Scriptures and examine the concise and profound teaching of Galatians 4:21–30. These verses illustrate what it looks like to live as "children of promise," born of the Spirit, or as slaves born "of the flesh" (vv. 23, 29). Many Muslims trace their lineage back to Hagar and Abraham's son, Ishmael, from whose line came Muhammad.[3]

The story unfolds in Genesis 16–18 and 21–22 that centers on Sarah and Hagar. Sarah struggles to become pregnant, so she gives her maidservant to her husband, Abraham, and she bears a son, Ishmael. God cares for Hagar and Ishmael and provides for them, but this is not the son God promised to Abraham. Instead, that son would be Isaac who was born through Sarah. This raises questions for Islam as their claimed forefather Ishmael is not the child of promise. In Galatians 4, we find these women again, used as an illustration of being in slavery to the law or being free in Christ. If we follow the logic of tracing roots to Ishmael and then to Abraham, this is not good news. It's slavery.

These thought-provoking verses are helpful to study with Muslim friends, verses which point out glaring differences between Christianity and Islam. Many Muslims believe it is enough that Abraham is a blood relation to them, or their peoples,[4] via Ishmael, but this isn't the son of the promise. Isaac is that promised son, and through his lineage comes Jesus, which means Jesus is the connection to Abraham in the sight of God!

DISCUSS AND REFLECT

1. Why do some people in society say there are multiple "Abrahamic religions"?

2. Biblically speaking, what makes us "Abrahamic"?

3. What is the danger of speaking of Islam as Abrahamic? (See Mark Durie's comments.)

4. What does Qur'an 5:32–33 teach, and how could it affect us?

5. How would you biblically counter Qur'an 5:33?

CHAPTER 4

Myth Four: Start with Islam in Evangelism

Remember the twenty-two-year-old missionary who sat muted in a refugee friend's North London council home? Soon after that I sat alongside three hundred Christians at a mission conference listening to a Westernized Arab Christian speak about Islam. He applied historical criticism against the Bible but failed to do the same against the Qur'an. An American missionary had just presented his approach to engaging and understanding Islam. He taught it was okay to leave Muslims inside Islam because they just needed to pray to Jesus as Lord; he admitted not all those "new believers" understood that Jesus is God. He believed the church was not essential and that Islam could accommodate Jesus-honoring communities.

At another conference, not long after, a British missional leader shared a vision he said he had received, which substantiated the positions of his Arab and American co-missionaries. Combined, their premise for understanding Islam was to look for our theological similarities and to use Islamic prayers alongside the Lord's Prayer.

I fell off my chair (not literally) when one of them stood to publicly slander Christianity as "a cold and cruel religion" then proclaimed: "Islam is a beautiful religion!"

HIS BOOKS CIRCULATE, STILL, through Christian colleges and mission schools.

Our starting point to understand and engage with Islam is still the Bible, even if we reference Qur'anic ideals in study and conversation. As we grow in the wisdom and knowledge of and from God (Prov. 2; Eph. 1:17), we compare all we see and witness to the Word of God.

By contrast, for some Christians, Islamic culture and religious practice become the foundation for how to witness among Muslims. Islamic texts inform their understanding of how to respond to Islam. Christian texts and theology are sometimes manipulated to conform to Islamic thinking, as if the mind of God needs approval from another religion. Christianity is often diluted to accommodate Islamic principles.

CULTURE AND RELIGION

Another pitfall awaiting some Christians is an attraction to new or communal lifestyles found within Islamic lands, which is not bad but becomes precarious if tied up with Islam.

Rituals and patterns are attractive to many Western Christians, and Islam has many. Certainly, a Christian Westerner settling in Turkey, Mali, or Pakistan learns new languages, eats local delicacies, and seeks to understand cultural traditions, but never should we manipulate our message to fit Islamic norms. A Christian's message stands apart from any culture. Eating delicious Afghani rice and meat stews on hygienically covered floors in refugee homes is not compromising our faith; it is just living as Jesus did—eating with "sinners" (Mark 2:13–17). Unlike Jesus, we too are sinners, but we know the One who is sinless, and eating with our neighbors is a great opportunity to tell them about Him! Just as we live within Western society, yet separate in values and holiness, so do we in Islamic lands. Our message in the West does not start with secularism; it starts with the living God. To be clear, culture can inform us as to words and styles of communication, but it should not compromise the person, or message, of the good news.

Some Christians may find Islamic culture and law attractive, especially compared with the Western church, which they deem distant and compromised. Sadly, in some instances there may be some truth to this conclusion, and it is likely the opinion behind the "Islam is beautiful" proclamation at that missionary conference. That said, we do not do away with church simply because there are some bad examples of it; there are enough good examples and biblical teaching to keep us on track in living as a community of believers within Islamic shores and among Muslims in the West.

Whatever the motive for starting with Islam for evangelism, the Bible—regardless of how faithful the church is or isn't in any given age—remains constant and faithful in its presentation of truth. Jesus remains the same "yesterday, today, and forever" (Heb. 13:8). The good news of Jesus does not change. He is relevant, transformative, and dynamic for every age, every situation, every person. If we lose sight of this, the Christian understanding of Islam becomes compromised.

JESUS IS OUR STARTING POINT

Are Jesus and the gospel powerful enough to change lives? Yes, He is, and it is. Start with Jesus. Then Islam does not seem so overwhelming, and gospel communication with Muslims becomes easier. In part because the person of Jesus challenges core aspects of Islamic teaching about God, salvation, and eternity. Starting with our favorite aspects of Jesus when we look at Islam cuts through the complexities of Islamic theology, history, and texts.

There is a difference between knowing about Islamic beliefs, which better help us understand our Muslim friend's mindset, and using Islam to explain the gospel. The latter can lead to confusion and being overwhelmed by the often changing[1] edicts of Islam. This is why starting with biblical wisdom will keep us walking in the "way of the good" and on "the paths of the righteous" (Prov. 2:20).

Recall the lists of what to do and not to do in those mission manuals? Many of those lists remain irrelevant and unhelpful, especially for a Western context. The example of Jesus, however, never ceases to provide inspiration for gospel engagement of Islam. Start with Jesus in evangelism among Muslims and witness how He works!

DISCUSS AND REFLECT

1. Biblically speaking, what is the foundation for how we engage Islam?

2. What pitfalls await Christians when they move into Islamic lands?

3. Why are some Christians drawn to Islamic ways?

4. How would you encourage a fellow Christian to stay on the "paths of righteousness"?

5. *Who* is our starting point as we engage Islam?

CHAPTER 5

Myth Five: Stay Away from Jesus, the Trinity, and the Old Testament

The first time a Muslim friend asked where the Trinity was taught in the Bible, I stumbled. Here was a Bible college grad unable to confidently point Muslim friends to one of the most important conversations a Christian can have with a Muslim. One about God! One that would clearly reveal that the Allah of the Qur'an is not the Creator of the heavens and earth, clearly revealed throughout the pages of the Bible. Did this show an unfamiliarity with the Scriptures, a lack of Bible depth and understanding? Had I fallen prey to the idea that the Trinity is too complicated to share with Muslims or Jesus was too confrontational for Islamic theology? Was I silencing myself by unhelpful evangelistic ideas? Yes. I believe so.

It certainly hit a cord of conviction and drove a newly prayed-over missionary to delve deep into the Scriptures, begin carrying a notebook filled with biblical and Qur'anic texts addressing multiple key differences between Islam and Christianity, Bible texts on the Trinity, divinity of Jesus, and view of the Scriptures, the life-giving Word of God. Then Qur'anic verses on the simplicity and oneness of Allah, denial of Jesus's (or Isa's) divinity, His crucifixion, and the Qur'anic views of revelation—very different from the way of Christ and His written Word.

I MAY HAVE STUMBLED through explaining the Trinity years ago, but after twenty-five years living among Muslim neighbors and teaching Christians about Islam, I've learned to begin with the Holy Trinity, Christ's divinity, and life-giving Bible revelation. We rejoice in the Trinity. We love the pages of the Bible. It breathes life into our evangelism among Muslims. It helps us understand Islam in a firm and grounded manner. It deepens our love for Muslims while understanding how vastly different our beliefs are to theirs.

Every age has had biblical prophets, kings, laws, and texts laying the same foundations to help us interact with a world torn by conflicting religious opinions. That foundation always leads us back to see the face of the invisible God (Col. 1:14–16). Note the obvious repetition here. That's because it is always helpful to keep repeating such truths when speaking with Muslims because though Isa was a fabulous person, or "spirit" (Q 21:91), in the Qur'an (Q 19:21, 30–31), its teaching about him hides the real Jesus from Muslims. He is given the title "Messiah" but devoid of its meaning (Q 4:171). In the Qur'an he is just a prophet alongside all the others (Q 2:136) and no eternal Son of God (Q 4:171–172). This is contrary to biblical teaching (Luke 24:46–49).

THE BIBLE'S STARTING POINT FOR UNDERSTANDING

After Muslim missionaries to Britain began challenging my Bible knowledge specifically on the topics of the Trinity and Jesus's divinity, I scoured the whole Bible for verses to learn and popped them into a little green book to pull out and read with Muslim friends. The following verses are a smattering of some of those and the kinds of verses that arise time and again in conversation.

Let's start with the New Testament's testimony of Jesus in the Old Testament. This is important because too many Muslims think the Old and New Testaments are not related in theology. We need to show how both speak of the same Lord and Savior of us all. The New Testament testifies to the *prebirth* creative work and existence of Jesus (John 1:1–3; 8:58; 17:5; Col. 1:1–2) and Old Testament teaching about Him (John 5:46–47; 17:5; Heb. 1:2–3, 8–12; Ps. 102:25–27). Muslims believe Jesus was created just two thousand years ago. Jesus says the Old Testament testifies about him. John 5:37–39 gives us a direct challenge from

Jesus to His listeners and to us the readers: "The Father who sent me has himself testified about me. You have not heard his voice at any time, and you haven't seen his form. You don't have his word residing in you, because you don't believe the one he sent. You pore over the Scriptures because you think you have eternal life in them, and yet they testify about me."

Wow! These verses are jam-packed full of insights. They tell us we don't currently see the heavenly Father. We are spiritually blind if we don't accept "the one" the Father sent (this is *not* Muhammad, though Muslims might say it is). We know the "sent one" is Jesus, and the Old Testament speaks about Him. Yet Muslims believe that Isa, their prophet, sent Muhammad after him, "When Jesus, the son of Mary, said, 'O children of Israel, indeed I am the messenger of Allah to you confirming what came before me of the Torah and bringing good tidings of a messenger to come after me, whose name is Ahmad'" (Q 61:6). They refer to John 14–16 as a proof text by replacing the Holy Spirit with Muhammad. This is partly done by manipulating the Greek word (which means "advocate/counselor"[1]) to mean "praised one," a word used for Muhammad. They also ignore the details given about the Holy Spirit within the same Scripture passages (John 14:26; 15:26; 16:7–15).

Jesus teaches us how the Old Testament speaks of Him: "He told them, 'These are my words that I spoke to you while I was still with you—that everything written about me in the Law of

Moses, the Prophets, and the Psalms must be fulfilled.' Then he opened their minds to understand the Scriptures" (Luke 24:44–45). Jesus implies there is much about Him within the books of Moses, the Prophets, and the Psalms.

Let's continue with this theme a bit more. Earlier in the chapter (Luke 24:25–27), Jesus makes another marvelous statement about all the Scriptures and prophets speaking of Him: "He said to them, 'How foolish you are, and how slow to believe all that the prophets have spoken! Wasn't it necessary for the Messiah to suffer these things and enter into his glory?' Then beginning with Moses and all the Prophets, he interpreted for them the things concerning himself in all the Scriptures." It certainly makes the Old Testament tantalizing! It means "all the prophets," starting with Moses, spoke of the person we call Jesus. It also crucially speaks about His suffering and glory. Muslims must contend with the fact that the prophets speak of the suffering of Christ and His glory, both of which Islam denies. Yet, even here, Muslim apologists such as Zakir Naik[2] from India will find ways to interpolate Muhammad onto this foretold person. Let's look at some of the many verses about the prophets of old meeting with our Lord and speaking of salvation through Him (Exod. 3; 33:11; 15:2).

- Genesis 16:10–13 introduces us to the Angle of the Lord to whom Sarah proclaims, "You are El-roi" for she said, "In this place, have I actually seen the one who sees me?" Many Old Testament seekers and believers realized they had seen God when the Angel of the Lord turned up to minister to them in person (Gen. 16:10–13; 22:11–14; Exod. 3:2, 14–15; Judg. 2:1–4; 2 Sam. 24:16). At other times, this visitor was called "the LORD" (Gen. 18:1; 31:11; 32:30; 48:15–16; 1 Sam. 3:7–10). Jacob's explanation provides clarity on these experiences, though the person he meets is called "a man" who also tells him he has struggled with God (Gen. 32:27–28), which Jacob understood, "'For I have seen God face to face,' he said, 'yet my life has been spared'" (Gen. 32:30). Moses often met the Lord: "The LORD would speak with Moses face to face, just as a man speaks with his friend" (Exod. 33:11). Who was this person they were meeting? It must be the Christ (Messiah). This can be a helpful conversation with Muslims, as they too speak of "the messiah" but remove the theological depths of what this title means. To be clear He is the anointed one from Heaven, God's Son, who comes to save (Psalm 2; John 20:28–31; Acts 13:32–41; Heb. 1–3). Allah never shows up and speaks directly with his people. Allah did not meet Islam's central prophet, Muhammad, to reveal the Qur'an; rather Islamic tradition says the Qur'an was "sent down" (*tanzil*) through an angel to Muhammad. We serve a God who has communicated directly with His people, both in time and space as He did with Moses, in His Word, and in Christ. Timothy (2 Tim. 3:15) is challenged to remember the sacred Scriptures of old, "which are able to give you wisdom for salvation through faith in Christ Jesus." Most of the New Testament hadn't been written when Timothy was growing up, which means the Old Testament is also "wise for salvation." This is a fabulous verse to read with Muslims because many Muslims believe the Old Testament's view of salvation is different from the New.

- The book of Acts gives us King David's testimony who tells us he "saw the Lord ever before me" and then worships the Lord by saying, "You will fill me with gladness in your presence" (Acts 2:25, 28). David's heart-filled praise is all about being in the presence of God, something which is amiss in Islam because being in the literal presence of Allah is not the goal of Islamic end-times theology. We will discuss this more in part 5.

- Jude 5 reminds us how "Jesus saved a people out of Egypt," from slavery and paganism in North Africa. The Lord personally led the people out of bondage and abuse. Jesus is emphatic about His ministry of setting people free when He quotes Isaiah 61:1–3 at the beginning of His ministry (Luke 4:16–21). Muslims might say Isaiah 61 is about Muhammad, but the verses are quite a contrast to Allah who informs Muslims to enslave others in war (Q 47:4), or in family life (Q 4:3, 24–25) evidenced by Muhammad (Q 33:52). Allah calls his people "my slaves" though he forgives their sins easily if they repent and turn to the "true faith" (Q 39:53–54). Unlike Christians, Muslims are not considered "children of God."

- Hebrews 11:26 reminds us that Moses gave up the treasures of Egypt to follow this Lord because "he considered reproach for the sake of Christ to be greater wealth than the treasures of Egypt." The whole chapter of Hebrews 11 to 12:3 is a wonderful summary of Old Testament faith and how they with us look unto Jesus. Many of them are claimed as Islamic prophets, but Muslims do not know about their relationship with God and God's saving work in their lives.

- First Corinthians 10:4 informs us of the thought-provoking truth of *who* the rock was upon which the ex-slaves from Northeast Africa were to rely. They were to trust this rock, who accompanied them, for provision and rebuilding their lives. This rock was Christ. We could leap into a comparison with Muhammad at this juncture and ask if he has been a rock for both ancient prophets and peoples past and present.

These verses are helpful starting places when studying the Bible with Muslims to seek a deeper understanding of how different it is to Qur'anic teaching. They highlight the hands-on relational work of God in history, and the importance of the Old Testament in understanding who God is, how God works, and how it all points to Jesus.

IN THE NAME OF THE TRINITY

Jesus's physical ministry concluded with the clearest of commands, which guides our every interaction with those who do not yet know Him—His Great Commission! (Matt. 28:19–20). When we work through each clause of this great command, it is helpful reading as we study Islam:

- "Go." Muslims often claim Jesus just came for the Jews. Here he was telling Jewish disciples to go out and tell the world about him.
- "Make disciples of all nations." Christianity is not limited to one language or centered on one city in Arabia like the practices of Islam. And it is not Western, which Muslims mistakenly presume.

- "Baptizing them in the name" distinguishes Christians from being disciples of Muhammad.
- "In the name of the Father and of the Son and of the Holy Spirit" challenges the being of Allah.
- "I am with you always, to the end of the age" begs the question if Muhammad would have been sent if God is already with us.

Clarity is here in full force about how we are to engage those who don't yet believe. The Lord Jesus tells us to start with Him—to focus on the Trinity and lead believers into biblical ways of thinking, committed to Christ's way, and proclaim the good news throughout the whole world. How bizarre it is to allow misguided teaching and our own fears and assumptions to guide us away from this last exhortation of Christ to the church! If God is who He says He is, and has given us all spiritual blessings through the Son in the power of the Spirit (Eph. 1:3), how can we keep this good news to ourselves? We must share it with our neighbors, including our Muslim neighbors. And how free we are in evangelism when our starting point is Jesus. He helps us understand the Trinity and the whole Scripture. He empowers us in discipleship, and He is the truth with whom we engage the unbelieving world!

DISCUSS AND REFLECT

1. What Bible verses spoke to you about God's relationship with us?

2. What Islamic belief clearly undermines biblical truth to you?

3. How would you challenge it with Scripture?

4. How do Islamic thinkers undermine John 14–16, and how would you correct it?

5. From this chapter, what Bible passage will you choose this week to memorize to aid your ability to witness for Jesus?

PART 2

Understanding Islam

CHAPTER 6

God Is Not Surprised by Islam

On a visit to a beautiful Christian college near the Mississippi River, a young man preached on Colossians 2, a passage which warns against philosophies and "empty deceit based on human tradition" (v. 8), religious diets, and new moon festivals that are based on the elements of the world, rather than Christ. As he read verses 8–23, he commented how it didn't seem applicable to us today, but still helpful "to learn from, when applied to equivalent scenarios from our culture."

True, and yet just thirty minutes away stood a grand and missional Islamic mosque, a house of prayer and center for Muslim communities, whose religious practices center around the cycle of the moon, prohibitions, human pagan traditions, and unbiblical religious practices. In essence, it followed "elements of the world" (v. 8).

What's more, a big portion of the secular society around him lived their days seeking prophecies found in astronomy, hoping the stars of the heavens could guide their daily habits and dreams.

Others dabble with tarot cards, occultism, and meditations—all dedicated to seasons, earth gods, man-made laws, prohibitions, and higher powers.

MANY YEARS LATER, HIS sermon is still relevant: Interest is high in witchcraft and New Age practices, and we see some similar elements in the religions around the world—Hinduism, Buddhism, and Islam. Which means the Bible passage in the young man's sermon directly addresses most non-Christian religions in the world today, as it has throughout history (Gal. 4:8–11).

The Bible challenges Islam's core doctrines and methods of religious practice, and the passage above is just one example of many. Yet how can we begin to understand Islam's core doctrines and practices? Most of us don't have hours in the day to pick up the Qur'an and read through its complex and unfamiliar commands, warnings, and fragmented stories.[1] When we look at the mass of Islamic writing, the writing to which Muslims turn to know about their religion, where do we begin? It can be overwhelming when first trying to grasp what Islam is, then navigate through the opinions, sometimes differing from one another, among our Muslim friends.

The solution is fabulous! The easiest way to begin understanding Islam, and Muslims, is to approach it, and its people, in the manner of Christ.

HOW DID JESUS ENGAGE UNBELIEVERS?

Jesus is known to have been asked more than two hundred questions in those thirty-three years gearing up to take our place on the cross. He asked many more, but we are currently not privy to them. Many of His questions were addressed to aggressive religious thinkers, or spiritually minded atheistic peoples. That means Jesus was speaking directly to the same kind of people living today.[2]

The Lord also asked the saints of old many questions. Consider His conversations with Abraham and Sarah, Hagar, Moses and Miriam, Samson's mother and father, Gideon and Isaiah, Zechariah, and Micah. Their interactions with God provide insight into the way biblical truth is communicated throughout the Scriptures. Compared with Islam's teaching about how Allah communicates with people, we find a God who visits[3] His people engages their ideas and deeply cares for them.

Islam is not different from the opposing religious ideals the Old Testament saints were grappling with. The gods they were tempted by and the seductions toward other mystical experiences are the same today. The Lord engages and confronts them, and the behavior that goes along with them, head on.

We gain a deeper understanding of Islam *when* we have an informed understanding of biblical engagement of false religion and cultural practices. That means reading our Bibles! We start with God's written Word!

THE BIBLE ADDRESSES ISLAMIC DOCTRINE

So, what does the Bible say of religions like Islam? Matthew 5–7 is a profound dissection of Islamic teaching. We do not need to know anything about Islamic doctrine; we only need to begin with Jesus's powerful sermon, open it with Muslim friends, and let the texts convict—Muslim and us alike—about our false gods and empty religious practices. This is a wonderful reality of the Bible as it challenges all of us!

Verses like those in Matthew 5–7 provide a deep analysis and understanding for topics of conversation with Muslim friends surrounding topics of prayer, fasting, false religion, morality, love, giving, and much more. Within this sermon we learn about:

- Biblical forgiveness (Matt. 5:38–41; 6:12–15) versus Islamic revenge (Q 16:126[4])

- Biblical love of neighbor and enemy (Matt. 5:43–48) versus Qur'anic edicts for aggression against enemies (Q 2:190–193)
- Discreet prayer (Matt. 6:5–13) versus the public shows of the Islamic ritualistic prayers (Q 4:102–103; 142–143; 5:6)
- Private fasting (Matt. 6:16–18) versus Islam's public monthlong fast[5]
- Biblical blessings on our persecutors (Matt. 5:9–12) versus Quranic encouragement to persecute (Q 5:33)

LOVING OUR NEIGHBORS AND ENEMIES

Where Christ tells us to love even our enemies (Matt. 5:4–6), the Qur'an teaches the opposite, especially toward non-Muslims, (Q 9:5, 29; 47:4). On occasion the Qur'an speaks of being kind to neighbors, but it is ambiguous about who "neighbors" are. "Worship Allah and associate nothing with Him, and to parents do good, and to relatives, orphans, the needy, the near neighbor, the neighbor farther away, the companion at your side, the traveler, and those whom your right hands possess [those you own]" (Q 4:36). However, when it speaks of specifics, such as "those who wage war against Allah and his messenger," it relates to anyone who challenges Islam, the Qur'an is clear: a violent response is required (Q 5:33; 9:5).[6]

Referencing Qur'anic verses can become complicated, as Islamic jurists will regard Islamic commentaries important for providing background information needed to understand the context of each Qur'anic verse. Some Muslims will say Qur'an 9:5 relates to a specific situation during the time of Muhammad. Whether this is true or not is debated. Regardless, the verse does provide insight into how Allah ordered those Muslims to treat non-Muslims: those they considered their enemies for breaking a treaty. Allah commanded them to lie in wait for them, ambush them, and kill them, or pay a tax, until they repented. A striking contrast to the last commands of Jesus to His disciples found in Matthew 28:19–20.

FORGIVING OUR NEIGHBORS AND ENEMIES

Where Christ tells us to forgive and leave vengeance to Him who judges justly (Deut. 32:35; Matt. 5:2), Islam teaches the opposite through vengeful edicts for Muslims to accomplish, (Q 5:33; 9:29), though forgiveness is also an option (Q 16:126; 42:40–43). Where Jesus tells us to be peacemakers (Matt. 5:9), the Qur'an tells us Allah and Muhammad will go to war with the unbelievers (Q 2:279). Qur'an 47:4 is clear in its response to non-Muslims: "When you meet those who disbelieve [in battle], strike [their] necks until, when you have inflicted slaughter upon them, then secure their bonds, and either [confer] favor afterwards or ransom [them] until the war lays down its burdens. That [is the command]. And if Allah had willed, He could have taken vengeance upon them [Himself], but [He ordered armed struggle] to test some of you by means of others. And those who are killed in the cause of Allah—never will He waste their deeds."[7] Some Muslims might point to other Qur'anic verses which show peacekeeping, though usually to fellow Muslims (Q 48:29), or ambiguous as to whom they are to be peaceful toward. When unbelievers, or enemies of Islam, are specifically addressed, ambiguity disappears, as we see in Qur'an 47:7.

SEEKING GOD

Where Jesus's life-changing sermon tells us His door will be thrown open for us if we seek Him (Matt. 7:7–12), Islam does not provide such assurance (Q 7:8–9). Having said that, Qur'anic verses like 48:29 imply forgiveness and reward, and though this is found in multiple places it is undermined by other verses. Qur'an 23:102–103 tells us that "those whose scales are heavy [with good deeds]—it is they who are the successful. But those whose scales are light—those are the ones who have lost their souls, [being] in Hell, abiding eternally." These good deeds are detailed throughout Islamic law, with their complexity leaving a Muslim unsure if their good deeds will outweigh their bad when they stand in judgment on the last day. What's more, since Allah is not described as consistent but does as he wills (Q 3:26), Muslims are left in a precarious position.

MIXED MESSAGES

As with many of its doctrines, the Qur'an does not teach a consistent message. Some Qur'anic verses say a person receives their due punishment or reward (Q 6:160; 28:84), but then good deeds can erase bad deeds (Q 2:271). Some verses show that good deeds will be enhanced on the scales of good and evil (Q 6:160; 64:17), but the same is said of bad deeds (Q 25:69; 41:27).

These contradictory ideas can be discussed with Muslim friends because Qur'anic verses do not provide a convincing answer, and the topic of conversation is wonderful for introducing the solution to this Qur'anic dilemma: the cross of Jesus. I'm so thankful the God of the Bible is unchanging and clear about the path to salvation through Jesus. Scales then become insignificant when we consider the work of Christ who deals with our sin head-on. Why bet on scales from Allah when assurance is found in Jesus!?

DISCUSS AND REFLECT

1. How did Jesus engage unbelievers?

2. How does Matthew 5–7 compare with the Qur'an?

3. What does Islam teach about neighbors and enemies?

4. What does Islam teach about salvation and assurance?

5. How is Jesus the solution to the mixed messaging of the Qur'an?

CHAPTER 7

Understanding Islam by Its Pillars and Beliefs

Mid conversation my Muslim friend stood up, put a shawl over her head, turned toward Mecca, and began to pray. Due to a language barrier, she didn't know how to excuse herself and explain what she was about to do, so I quietly retreated and went to see if I could help in the kitchen. After her long recitations of prayer, she began to wail, begging Allah to hear her personal prayers. She had just completed the "salat" (formal prayers) and was now able to present her personal prayer (dua). I quietly prayed in the name of Jesus, knowing that my prayers went directly to my heavenly Father, but knew she was not sure if her prayers were heard. Confidence in knowing our prayers are heard may be seen as arrogant by some Muslims, and it would be if it were reliant on our own works. Yet it is only possible because of Jesus, and this is something I longed to share with my dear friend. She was pious and committed, for hours working through her row of ninety-nine prayer beads (called subha or dhikr beads), keeping Islamic practices precisely, breaking the fast at the exact time Mecca allowed, saying the right statements, fearful if anyone in the family strayed. There was something convicting about her dedication, yet all to a god she can't be sure has heard her prayers.

THE REQUIREMENTS OF THE Islamic law may lead us to ask if it has become a mantle of slavery, which stands in contrast to the relationship of trust and friendship with the living God we find in Jesus's Sermon on the Mount (Matt. 5:44; 6:9, 26, 30; 7:11). The Qur'an leaves out this key element of biblical law and presents a law that has no relationship with the God behind it. My pious Muslim friend was locked into her rituals and worked earnestly to receive reward and paradise. Her motives to connect to God were right, but her religion drew a barrier between her and the Lord.

Islam teaches "right intention" of its followers (Qur'an 2:225; 24:64), meaning Muslims must have honorable intention when fulfilling their religious practices. Their practices shouldn't be devoid of meaning. It also teaches righteousness, which comes from having correct Islamic beliefs (Q 2:177). But it is all devoid of friendship with God. Islam's practices leave out this key element of biblical truth—relationship and delight of the Lord, which then makes us outward looking to the needs of those around us, rather than seeking reward.

ISLAM'S FIVE, OR SIX, PILLARS *(DEEN)*

I have read books which laid out the five (or six) pillars of Islam, but what does *pillar* mean for Muslims? Looking back, none of my Muslim friends use the word *pillar*, although they do refer to their practices, which we describe as "pillars." They use the word *deen* to reference faithful Islamic practice. Islamic prayer and fasting were at the heart of my friend's religious practice, and her pilgrimage to Mecca often became a topic of conversation, as well as the charity her family must give, usually during Ramadan. The specific statement of faith—the *Shahadah*—is rarely discussed, though a Muslim must believe in Allah and Muhammad.

These pillars: Islamic fasting (called *sawm*), Islamic formal prayers (*salat*), Islamic financial giving (*zakat*), and the once-in-a-lifetime pilgrimage to the city of Mecca in Saudi Arabia (*hajj*), are imbued with a specific statement of belief proclaiming Allah as God and Muhammad as his prophet (the *Shahadah*[1]). Both those beings, Allah and Muhammad, do not teach the way of Jehovah.

Fasting Acceptable to God

The Old Testament is full of verses like those in Matthew 5–7.

Take Isaiah 58, which is a succinct presentation of what is behind biblical fasting. When we compare it with the Islamic monthlong fast, which Muslims must accomplish once in their lifetime to try to atone for their sins, we see how Islamic practice moves away from God's ways. This is because a key element of biblical fasting and prayer is undermined in Islamic practice—holy living and relationship with the Lord Jesus. That relationship is then evidenced in the Christians' generous and sacrificial lives lived within community. Biblical fasting looks to others, while Islamic fasting looks to self and the hope of acceptance by Allah.

Jesus's teaching on fasting stands in stark contrast to the exhibition of Islam's monthlong fast, Ramadan. Ramadan is about appeasing Allah, with the hope of access into postlife gardens, while biblical fasting is quiet communion with our heavenly Father. It is also serving and caring for others (Isa. 58). While I do not keep the Islamic fast—because it is a core Islamic practice to a god I do not believe in, and I do not wish to confuse my Muslim friends—it can be a joy to join them for the meal as they break their fasts each night after sundown and an adventure to discuss the differences between Christian practice and

Islamic. Topics of forgiveness, faithfulness to God, and reasons for our practices open wide doors to deep conversations about the Lord. Feasting with Muslim friends is fun and a wonderful community experience. We may not agree with their religion, but we love living life with them.

Isaiah 58 calls out religious hypocrisy and empty religious ritual. Likewise, Jesus called out hypocrisy among scribes and religious leaders in the New Testament (Mark 12:38–40; Luke 18:9–14). We read in Isaiah 58 a list of empty religious practice in the sight of God: oppression of workers, strife, fistfights, judgments, and slander, ignoring the gift of a Sabbath rest, seeking our own amusements first (vv. 4, 9, 13). Biblical fasting leads to humility, freedom from slavery, help for sinners toward holiness, generosity of food, homes for homeless, clothes for the naked, care for the family. The Lord will hear our prayers, heal us, and be a light in the darkness. Our lands will replenish, our cities will be restored, and we will be part of God's work to heal our lands (vv. 11–12).

Prayer

Just as there are differences between Islamic and biblical fasting, the same applies to prayer. Where Jesus tells us to pray in private, without show, the formal Islamic prayers are recited in public (Matt. 6:5–6; Q 2:238; 4:102). Although the Qur'an does not give all the details of how to pray, those are found in Islamic law. Where Jesus teaches us to pray to our heavenly Father, to acknowledge His kingdom, and to forgive as we wish to be forgiven (Matt. 6:9–14), Islam's recital prayer speaks of Allah, and according to Islamic commentators denounces Jews and Christians in verse 7 of Qur'an 1. This prayer is called the *Fathah*, meaning "the opening," and is at the heart of Islam's daily ritual prayers. It does not speak of a friendship with Allah, and Muslims would not address Allah as "Abba, Father" (Rom. 8:15).

Charity

A Muslim friend might say, "Charity is a key Islamic practice," and point to an increase in charitable giving during Islam's monthlong fast. Though the Qur'an speaks of charity, it does not provide Muslims with the knowledge of how to give. The details are found in Islamic law and are quoted verbatim throughout Islamic charitable websites. Online forums are filled with Muslims asking how much and what to give. Beneath the need to get it right lies the fear that Allah must approve of the giving if a person is to be accepted by him and hope for reward in this life and the afterlife. So, what kind of "intention" do Muslims have when they give? Is it to give abundantly to bless others and be an extended arm of the generosity of God or to seek reward for self?

Islam's Pilgrimage

When our Muslim friends enthusiastically describe their pilgrimage (*Hajj*) to Mecca in Saudi Arabia, it sounds pagan to the Christian mind. Their pilgrimage (Q 3:97) rituals include practices seen in pre-Islamic Arabia, such as throwing stones at the devil or standing on mountains all night long, circling and kissing a meteorite at the heart of a cubed house called the Khaba. For Christians, pilgrimage is a call to gather and learn (Deut. 31:11; Acts 2:5–11), gather and worship (2 Chron. 30:1), and walk in the path of the Lord (Isa. 2:3). Gatherings and festivals in the Bible lead God's people to song and gladness (Isa. 30:29) and a new intimacy with the Lord.

Muslims who have completed the pilgrimage to Mecca refrain from singing and dancing. Laughter is to be kept at a minimum, and the demure formality of the new "hajji"[2] receives respect from the community. Behavior may differ from person to person, but lists of guidance on correct behavior is found in Islamic traditions and sayings of Muhammad. By contrast, each week Christians make their "pilgrimage" to church to sing together and draw near to the Lord (Eph. 5:19–20). Each day Christians set time aside to draw close to the Lord in prayer and conversation (Ps. 1:1–6; 119:9–16). Though we are called to gather often, there is no need to go on a specific pilgrimage to appease God to receive blessing for now and the afterlife.

Qur'anic Jihad

For some Muslims, there is a further practice, one of *jihad*, contradicting Isaiah 58 and Matthew 5–7 but clearly taught in Muhammad's key sermon found in Qur'an 9. Within Islam there are debates about what *jihad* means. Traditionally, and *in* Islamic law, jihad is striving against the enemies of Islam, namely through forms of violence. For those who reject this understanding (mostly Westernized or "progressive" Muslims), it is a form of internal striving, a person's struggle against sin within. They would turn to verses such as Qur'an 22:78, "And strive for Allah with the striving due to Him. . . . So establish prayer and give zakah and hold fast to Allah." Two other verses supporting 'internal striving' arise in conversation with Muslims, Qur'an 5:32 and 33:35. So perhaps both versions of jihad can be gleaned from Islamic texts, although a historical emphasis on violent jihad is prominent, and it is certainly prevalent in the Qur'an (Q 9:73; 9:111). Disabled people are exempt from doing jihad, though the verse is clear that Allah prefers those who fight "in the cause of Allah" (Q 4:95). The life of Muhammad affirms a violent engagement of unbelievers (Q 9:73, 88).

To understand the Qur'an, Muslims refer to literature (such as the interpretations of the Qur'an, called Tafsir, and the biographies of Muhammad, called Sira) usually written hundreds of years later to provide a background context for every Qur'anic verse. Regardless of context, the following words do not fit with the teaching of Jesus in His Sermon on the Mount: "Fight those who do not believe in Allah or in the Last Day and who do not consider unlawful what Allah and His Messenger have made unlawful and who do not adopt the religion of truth from those who were given the Scripture—[fight] until they give the jizyah willingly while they are humbled"[3] (Q 9:29). It is difficult to glean an "internal jihad" from the many verses like this. That said, having discussions with Muslim friends about sin can be fruitful, especially when linked with Jesus as the solution!

The Shahadah

Islam's practices are undergirded by Islam's statement of faith: "I bear witness that there is no God but Allah, and Muhammad is the Messenger of Allah." The statement comes from a variation of it found on the Dome of the Rock in Jerusalem, the possible birthplace of Islam.[4] In practice, not only is Muhammad to be acknowledged alongside Allah, but he is also to be obeyed alongside Allah: "And obey Allah and the Messenger that you may obtain mercy" (Q 3:132). To convert to Islam, a person must say the Shahadah. Not only is it a statement of faith, but it is also a statement that denies any other god and any other prophet, both of whom do not belong to Christianity.

ISLAMIC BELIEFS

When I first started learning Islamic theology at Bible college, little biblical engagement had found its way into Christian books explaining Islamic tenets of faith, and so I felt a little stuck. How do I *biblically* engage Islamic beliefs? I questioned why so few books I had read thus far had provided a clear biblical alternative to the pillars, beliefs, and history of Islam.

Thankfully some helpful books today aid Christians to quickly grasp key elements of Islam.[5] So we will not go into too much detail here, though we do want to biblically engage with Islam's six core beliefs. This is important because supposed similarities with Christianity are still included in texts addressing Islam.[6]

THE SIX ISLAMIC BELIEFS *(IMAN)*

All mainstream Muslims affirm the six core beliefs of Islam:

1. belief in one God
2. angels (and jinn, which are spirit beings and demons)
3. Islamic prophets
4. books of Allah
5. divine decrees (fatalism)
6. judgment day

They sound biblical at first glance, but when a Muslim speaks about them, what do they mean? Does the Qur'an speak in detail about them? And do they align with the Bible? Not at all. Take the Islamic belief of "prophets." Islam reveres the prophets such as Adam, Noah, Abraham, Moses, and David. But note this: though some Islamic prophets may be similar in name, they are not similar in theology or in the details of their stories and certainly not in their relationship with God.

The beliefs of Islam intermingle with almost any topic of theology, and they will appear throughout the book. When we consider Muhammad, the Qur'an, salvation, mystical practices, and end times, think about this key list of Islamic theology. Just like Christians, Muslims are serious about correct doctrine.

The word *deen* appears multiple times in the Qur'an connected to right practice (such as not eating pork): "This day I have perfected for you your religion (your deen) and completed My favor upon you and have approved for you Islam as religion" (Q 5:3). The word is also connected to right belief, the religion of Allah, obedience, and judgment: "Indeed, the religion in the sign of Allah is Islam. And those who were given the Scripture did not differ except after knowledge had come to them. . . . And whoever disbelieves in the verses of Allah, then indeed, Allah is swift in [taking] account" (Q 3:19). Practice and belief are intertwined in many Qur'anic verses.

SEEING ISLAM THROUGH A BIBLICAL GRID

When we fear the Lord Jesus and love His Word, we will see how different Islam is from the truth. When we see Islam through a biblical grid, we gain understanding and can answer Islamic questions about life, God, and eternity. Engage Islam, as Jesus engaged false religions, and we are empowered to witness among Muslims.

I recall a Bible-loving missionary from Northwest Africa, stating with clarity and confidence at an American missionary conference, "On all core points of the gospel, Islam teaches the opposite." Note his statement starts with the gospel—a good place to start. Then compare Islamic theology to it.

DISCUSS AND REFLECT

1. What is different between Islamic and biblical law?

2. What are the five pillars (*deen*) of Islam?

3. What is the Shahadah, and why do Christians disagree with it?

4. How can we biblically respond to Islam's pillars?

5. What are the six core beliefs (*iman*) of Islam?

CHAPTER 8

Understanding Islam by Its Texts

A Pakistani Muslim missionary had just arrived in the UK to join the focused mission field Muslims had on the country. From the UK, Islamic literature was distributed into Europe, and Islamic teachers taught worldwide at mission training centers and online. American-style Christian apologetic resources were converted into Islamic, and what looked like plagiarized Islamized material filled the stalls and book tables, placed by Muslim missionaries along busy city streets both stateside and in Europe.

The newly arrived missionary loudly told me that "the Bible was corrupted!" He leveled all the normal challenges taught in every Western jamaat (mosque) across the land, or so it seemed, and we embarked on a fun discussion about the Bible. Toward the end, it was time to start asking questions about the Qur'an, which he believed was perfect and unchanged. I mentioned to him that I had two different Arabic Qur'ans that were not exactly alike and a copy of one of the oldest Qur'ans in my bag. I pulled out the heavy tome and opened it up to pages containing summaries from the two Islamic Turkish scholars who had studied it. Clear as day they acknowledged differences and discrepancies between this Qur'an and other early Qur'ans. The eyes of the Muslim missionary looked bewildered, as tears brimmed up. The mirage in his mind of a perfect Qur'an had begun to crumble. Not through any words of my own, but by simply seeing the latest research for himself, he saw how his beloved Qur'an had been changed and had the same sorts of issues any ancient text has.

It is not the miracle he thought it was.

MOST OF THE INFORMATION about Islamic books and what they teach comes from Islamic traditions and their view of history. Actual history will tell a different story, but it is good to understand Islam from the perspective of Muslims so that you know what they consider important as they apply their religion to their lives. Before we consider the texts of Islam, let's look at the different factions within Islam because they follow different variations of their texts. In this section we'll focus on two main groups of Muslims: Sunni and Shi'ah Muslims.

Sunni Muslims follow writings they believe have come from Muhammad and the four leaders after him whom leaders call "the rightly guided Caliphs"—Abu Bakr, the father of Muhammad's child bride, Aisha; Umar, one of his companions; Uthman, who is credited with compiling the verses of the Qur'an from many different sources in the mid-seventh century; and Ali, part of Muhammad's family. This is where the divide between Sunni and Shi'a Islam comes in. Whereas Sunni Muslims follow caliphs in the ilk of the first four caliphs, Shi'a follow leaders from the line of Muhammad. For them there are twelve Imams. The last one is now miraculously hiding and will one day return.

THE BOOKS OF ISLAM

A religion and its practice are ultimately understood through its founder and its revelation. For Islam, according to its traditions, that's Muhammad (Q 33:21; 48:8–9) and the Qur'an (Q 16:89; 41:2–6). Yet there are five more collections of books Muslims traditionally deem authoritative:

1. the sayings and behavior of Muhammad (*Hadith*)
2. the biographies of Muhammad (the *Sira*)
3. the commentaries of the Qur'an (*Tafsir*)
4. the histories of Islam (*Tarikh*)
5. the Islamic law (*Shari'ah law*)

The vast tomes of Islamic books and writings can make understanding Islam overwhelming and inaccessible, as does the emphasis on Arabic being the language of Allah. For example, when Muslims quote the Qur'an, it is only considered the Qur'an if it is recited in Arabic. Other language versions are considered interpretations or copies of the "noble Qur'an." They also reference the Arabic name of Qur'anic chapters (sometimes called books) or refer to each chapter as a "surah." Western scholars use numerical references, and for ease we will do the same. For example, we write Qur'an 8:12, while Muslims say surah 8:12 or al-Anfal 8:12.

SUNNI ISLAMIC LAW[1]

The diverse factions of Islam hold different texts as authoritative. Sunni Islam, which describes most Muslims, generally see the above texts as their own. They follow one of the four main schools of Islamic law, which are named after their founder:

1. Hanafi (d. AD 767), from Kufa, Iraq

   - popular in Central Asia, Russia, Turkey, Northern Arabia
   - The Taliban of Afghanistan and the Deobandi of India lean toward Hanafi law.

2. Maliki (d. AD 795), from Medina, Saudi Arabia
   - popular in North and Northwest Africa

3. Shafi'i (d. AD 820), from Gaza, Palestine
   * popular in East Africa, Shi'ah areas of the world and Southeast Asia

4. Hanbali (d. AD 855), from Baghdad, Iraq
   * popular in Saudi Arabia
   * strict adherence to the Qur'an and Hadith made famous by Ibn Taymiyyah (d. AD 1328) leading to what the West call "Wahabism," though they view themselves as Salafis.

SALAFI ISLAM

We need to briefly note Salafism because it supersedes all the schools of Islamic law. Within all the factions of Islam is the tension between how literal a Muslim follows the Qur'an and life of Muhammad. "There has certainly been for you in the Messenger of Allah an excellent pattern for anyone whose hope is in Allah and the Last Day" (Q 33:21). Sometimes seen as revivalist movement, Salafis follow an Islamic legal and theological school that strictly adheres to the literal text (*zāhir*) of the Qur'an and Hadith as the only source of Islamic law. A committed Christian who loves the Bible will understand this movement, as we too see the Bible and the Lord Jesus as the foundation of how to build our lives. In a similar vein, Salafis see Muhammad and the Qur'an as their foundation. They are rooted in their texts.

To Salafis the first generations of Muslims are pious predecessors who are to be emulated, as directed by the Qur'an (Q 9:100). Salafi Muslims have always existed, contrary to the beliefs of some modern commentators, because they follow a basic, foundational Islam easy to support from its texts. Jurist and theologian Ibn Taymiyyah (d. 1328) sought to bring Muslims back to the way of Muhammad in the Middle Ages, and Islam rose again as the Ottoman empire declined and Saudi influence increased from the twentieth century.[2] This later movement is referred to as "Wahabi" Islam by Western pundits, though it is not a name Muslims would use to define themselves.

IMPLEMENTING ISLAMIC LAW

Arabic words are at the heart of understanding Islamic law and how it works. As with any law in the world, experts are needed to interpret it, but the different Islamic schools have methods for understanding jurisprudence when edicts are not clear from the Qur'an or Muhammad's life. Let's look at Maliki law for an example. As jurists consider law, the Qur'an is their first stop, but if it is not clear (as is often the case), then customs and traditions long held within the Islamic community and the practices of Muhammad found in the Hadith are considered. If no help is found there, then they will turn to the rulings from the four first caliphs. Each school of law has a different method of deriving law, with varying levels of flexibility. Hanbali law being the strictest (rulings) of the four schools. The texts of Islamic law, or modern fatwas derived from them, drive the daily lives of many Muslims.

SUNNI HADITH COLLECTIONS

The sayings and actions of Muhammad are incredibly important to Muslims, and when Muslims write about Islam or comment on how to be Muslim, they are referring to the Hadith. According to Islamic belief, each Hadith collection contains statements from Muhammad, his companions or family (the latter is important for Shi'ah Muslims), and early Islamic jurists.

1. Sahih Bukhari ("collected"[3] by Bardizbah al-Juʿfī al-Bukhārī, d. AD 870); includes 7,275 Hadith
2. Sahih Muslim (collected by Muslim b. al-Hajjaj, d. AD 875); includes 9,200 Hadith

3. Sunan Abu Dawood (collected by Abu Dawood, d. AD 888); includes 4,800 Hadith

4. Jami al-Tirmidhi (collected by al-Tirmidhi, d. AD 892); includes 3,956 Hadith

5. Sunan al-Sughra (collected by al-Nasa'i, d. AD 915); includes 5,279 Hadith

6. Sunan ibn Majah (collected by Ibn Majah, d. AD 887); includes more than 4,000 Hadith

Then there is the al-Muwatta (the Approved) of Malik (collected by Imam Malik, d. AD 795); 1,720 hadith. Many Muslims read this collection.

The hadith rely on a trail of narrations passed from generation to generation until they are written down. To decide if a hadith is sound (*sahih*), it must have a connected chain of transmission back to the person who made the initial statement. That person must be considered upright and with reliable narrations free from flaws. Some hadith are rejected if they are deemed weak (*da'if*), usually meaning they can't be traced back to Muhammad or those around him, or the "narrator" is suspect. And then there is a take-it-or-leave-it response to hadith considered "good" (*hasan*). There is more to it, with different opinions, and it becomes incredibly complex. Muslim scholars spend years studying this Islamic "science."

SHI'A[4] ISLAM

Shi'a[5] Muslims, found mainly in Iran, Iraq, and Syria, would reject many Sunni Hadith, and look to the writings of their sacred twelve Imams, the last one of whom is alive but hidden and will return as a messiah-type figure. Shi'a Muslims see themselves as "people of the house" (*ahl al-bayt*). Their leaders are Imams who are descendants of Muhammad, which is semi supported by the Qur'an: "Indeed, Allah chose Adam and Noah and the family of Abraham and the family of 'Imran over the worlds—Descendants, some of them from others" (Q 3:33–34). They possess special spiritual and political authority and have come to be seen as infallible and divinely ordained.[6] The twelve are:

1. Ali (d. AD 661), the Commander of the Believers (al-Mu'minin, also called al-Murtaza)[7]
2. Hasan (d. AD 670), the Chosen (al-Mujtaba)
3. Hussein (d. AD 680), the Master of Martyrs (al-Shuhada)
4. Zayn (d. AD 712), the one who Constantly Prostrates/Worshiper of Allah (al-Sajjad)

5. Muhammad (d. AD 733), the One Who Opens Knowledge (al-Baqir)
6. Ja'far (d. AD 765), the Truthful (as-Sadiq)
7. Musa (d. AD 799), the Calm One (al-Kazim)
8. Ali (d. AD 817), the Pleasing One (al-Reza/Rida)
9. Muhammad (d. AD 835), the God-fearing (al-Jawad)
10. Ali (d. AD 868), the Guide (al-hadi)
11. Hassan (d. AD 874), the Citizen of a Garrison Town (al-Askari)
12. Muhammad (alive and hidden), the Guided, the Hidden One (al-Mahdi)

Shi'a Muslims may follow some of the laws of Sunni Islam because they all share Muhammad, but they primarily look to the above Imams, with multiple sects of Islam developing from the teachings of the different Imams. The sermons of Ali ibn Abi Talib, the fourth "rightly guided caliph" are at the heart of Shi'a thinking and captured in a collection of his sermons called "the Path of the Eloquence" (*Nahj al-Balaghah*).[8]

THE SUNNAH

A quick note on the *Sunnah*, an important word for Muslim jurists. Sunnah (meaning "habitual practice") largely refer to the habitual practice of Muhammad. His words, actions, permissions, and prohibitions found in the Hadith. Sunnah are those things which influence and guide a Muslim's daily life from religious ritual to daily ablutions. If Muhammad used a twig (*miswak*) to clean his teeth, then so can Muslims today. Sunnah are used as a basis for legal rulings. They are at the heart of how Salafi Muslims live their lives.

ISLAMIC VIEW OF OUR TEXTS

When Muslims speak about God's revelation to Christians, they may refer to the Torah and the Injil. The Qur'an teaches that each generation received a revelation for its time until the Qur'an, which is the final revelation. If asked where the Injil is today, most Muslims say it has been lost. They believe the former "revelations" agree with one another and the Qur'an (Q 3:3; 5:46; 57:27), but if there are differences, then the Qur'an is always right, even if historical evidence proves otherwise. Qur'an 7:157 makes a startling claim about "the messenger" (Muhammad in Muslim minds) mentioned in the Torah and the Gospels. Our texts are then scoured for references of Muhammad. If he can't be found, or if it is different from the Qur'an, then the Bible is deemed by Muslims as "corrupted." Although the Qur'an does not say that the Bible has been corrupted. If the conversation ever comes up, I always ask my Muslim friends who corrupted it, where, and when? None know the answer, though some will refer to the Council of Nicaea in the early fourth century as the culprit. I remind my friends that we do not claim the Bible was "handed down"; rather it was written through the pens of God's people who were inspired by the Lord or spoke with the Lord face-to-face (as with Moses), or in visions and dreams (as with Ezekiel), and now through His Son (Heb. 1:1–3), in multiple locations covering huge epochs of history. Muhammad simply met an angel or an "unnamed being who was mighty in power," who told him to "recite" (Q 73:4; 96:1–5; 53:5–12).[9] Muslims believe the Qur'an was handed down (*tanzil*) to Muhammad and is preserved (Qur'an 15:9; 85:21–22).

Muslims will find sectarian Christian literature to support their views, such as the Gospel of Barnabas or the Gospel of Judas, and claim they contain the correct version of history, not the Bible. With a little bit of knowledge, these claims are easy to discredit. The Gospel of Barnabas was written in Italian and Spanish, dated to the thirteenth to fifteenth century, and denies Jesus's crucifixion. In it Jesus denies His divinity and mentions Muhammad. Judas died in his place instead, which fits with Qur'an 4:157, "They did not kill him, nor did they crucify him; but [another] was made to resemble him to them." It is not part of the biblical record, written far too late and obviously an Islamic apologetic.[10]

THE WRITTEN AND LIVING WORD OF GOD

Like Islam, Christianity is understood through the *written* Word, the Bible (Heb. 4:12). Unlike Islam, it is also understood through personally knowing the *living* Word, the Lord Jesus (John 1:1–14; Heb. 1:1–3). When all else fails, Jesus is our answer to everything! As a stark contrast to Him, let's continue to peruse the Qur'an and traditions of Islam and see how Muhammad stands in lifestyle and rituals.

DISCUSS AND REFLECT

1. What two sets of leaders do Sunni and Shi'a Muslims follow?

2. List the six core writings of traditional Sunni Islam.

3. What are the four schools of Sunni Islamic law?

4. What is Salafi Islam, and why might Christians understand it?

5. How do Muslims view the Bible, and how would you answer them?

CHAPTER 9

Understanding Islam by Its Prophet

A former Muslim met the Lord through reading the whole Bible. It made a profound impact on his life. He is a hafiz, a person who can recite the whole Qur'an. The Qur'an is about the size of the New Testament. As a Muslim he could recite the Qur'an in multiple languages; he still can. When he teaches Islam, he quotes Qur'anic verses in Arabic, translating each one as he narrates.

His classes are excellent, and during one of his Qur'anic classes, we were learning how to interpret the Qur'an as a Muslim jurist would interpret it. Hearing two hours of Qur'anic recitation makes for uncomfortable listening and an unsettledness in the Christian spirit. Our teacher concluded his class by simply and boldly stating: "Muhammad came to undermine and undo the work of Christ! Now you understand Islam for what it is. Go out and introduce Muslims to Christ."

AS A HAFIZ AND Islamic law expert, our Qur'an teacher was a highly revered Muslim, who moved in the courts of Islamic law. As a Christian he still carries in his mind the Qur'an, a book bent on undermining the Savior he so loves. He has since filled his mind with biblical truth to counter the Qur'anic words that lie inside, and now he boldly proclaims Christ as God and Savior. Speaking about Islam as clearly as he does might make some people uncomfortable, yet he is a clear thinker helping fellow Christians understand "Islam for what it is."

ISLAM'S MESSIAH

Many people put Islam into a special category, as if it is a new religion, one the Bible cannot possibly understand. Yet Islam is simply another religious view that is addressed throughout the Scriptures, just under a different name.

Islam teaches about the Christ, the Messiah, but their messiah is not our Messiah (Q 5:116), and he has been given a different name: Isa. He is created, like Adam, without an earthly father (Q 3:59) and is concerned about denying his divinity. Dr. Bernie Power, speaker and author on Islam, has drawn up a detailed list of Qur'anic teachings that parallel the Bible in relation to his birth, titles, humanity, miracles, revelation, special role, and followers.[1] Though Isa is significant in the Qur'an and mentioned by name far more times than Muhammad, Muhammad has become Islam's central person through whom religious life should be understood the former Islamic jurist's statement, "Muhammad came to undermine and undo the work of Christ," is spot-on when it comes to understanding how Islam responds to the biblical Jesus.

Let's stay with some helpful comparisons on these topics. If the details seem overwhelming as we go deeper into the issues, sticking to a simple comparison between Jesus and Muhammad cuts through the wealth of material available for investigation.

COMPARING JESUS AND MUHAMMAD[2]

The Qur'an repeatedly calls Allah's followers to obey "the messenger." Though Muhammad is only mentioned four times by name in the Qur'an (Q 3:144; 33:40; 47:2; 48:29), today the messenger means Muhammad. If you disobey Muhammad, you are put into the "unbeliever" category (Q 3:21, 31–32; 4:13–14, 59, 79–80; 24:56; 33:36). He is the role model for Muslims (Q 33:21), and what he forbids or gives must be accepted (Q 59:7). Good deeds are understood by many Muslims through the life of Muhammad. His actions aid Muslims in Islamic behavior, though most of it is not found in the Qur'an, which is why the other books are important. Since good deeds and practices are understood through the life and teaching of Muhammad, let's briefly contrast his example and teaching with Jesus's sermon on the Mount (Matthew 5–7).

Good Deeds

In Islam good deeds are for personal gain, or the good of the Muslim community. The Qur'an emphasizes Islamic practices as deeds (Q 33:35) and details what Muslims can and can't do (Q 4:23–25). Muslims pursue these deeds with the hope of a better afterlife. The Bible also has lists, but they read differently from Islam and have more to do with character or ethical and moral choices (Gal. 5:19–26; 2 Pet. 1:5–7). Both books give consequences for sin (Rev. 21:8; Q 101:8–11), though their views shouldn't be equated. For example, immorality is not consistent in Islam (Q 4:3; 33:50).

Those who are "with Muhammad" are to be forceful against disbelievers but merciful to fellow Muslims. "Muhammad is the Messenger of Allah; and those with him are forceful against the disbelievers, merciful among themselves. You see them bowing and prostrating [in prayer], seeking bounty from Allah and [His] pleasure. Their mark is on their faces from the trace of prostration.[3] . . . Allah has promised those who believe and do righteous deeds among them forgiveness and a great reward" (Q 48:29).

For Christians, goodness stems from knowing Christ and being a light in the world so that all can see our good deeds and praise our Father in heaven (Matt. 5:14–16). Good deeds are toward *all* people and point to God, not to us, and these deeds are not necessary for our salvation.

Purity and Holiness

Purity and holiness point to God's beauty, but holiness and purity fall short in Islam. For example, where Jesus commands holy living and faithfulness to our spouse (Matt. 5:27–32), Muhammad and the Qur'an teach the opposite. Qur'an 4:3, 25, teach polygamy or the taking of women as sex slaves (described as "those your right hand possesses") and Muhammad's example in Qur'an 33:37, when Allah helps him marry his adopted son's wife, provide some examples of this. See also Allah's threats of divorce to Muhammad's wives who did not obey him in Qur'an 66:1–5.

Treasures

Where Jesus tells us not to build up treasures on earth (Matt. 6:19–24), Muhammad lived a life filling his pockets with loot from enemies. We find these details in the earliest Islamic biographies of Muhammad, called the *sira*. These details are not found in modern Western editions of Muhammad's story, but they are found in the earliest detailed stories from history and in accounts from witnesses of the time.[4]

Kingdoms

Where Jesus tells us to seek God's kingdom, from where all provision comes (Matt. 6:25–34), Islam teaches a different kingdom that has a different aim, based on obedience to Muhammad (Q 4:59; 33:31), Islamic beliefs and rule (Q 2:30; 6:165), and a mighty earthly empire. Qur'an 24:55 speaks of "succession . . . upon the earth" granted to those who believe in Allah and Islamic good works, with an emphasis on "not associating anything with [Allah]." As with prayer, the Islamic political and religious kingdom is not detailed in the Qur'an but expounded in the Islamic law and gleaned from the example of Muhammad's life.

Judging and Judgment

Where Jesus tells us not to judge (Matt. 7:1–6; Rom. 14:10), in part because he is the judge (John 5:22; Rev. 19:11), the Qur'an and Muhammad demand judgment on nonbelievers, with the judgment sometimes including violent retribution (Q 2:191; Q 9:5, 73). Remember those who are with Muhammad "are forceful against the disbelievers."

False Prophets

What's more, Jesus's warning of false prophets in Matthew 7:13–23 describes Muhammad's life and religion found in the earliest Islamic biographies and the Qur'an. "Be on your guard against false prophets who come to you in sheep's clothing but inwardly are ravaging wolves. You'll recognize them by their fruit" (Matt. 7:15–16). Muhammad's fruit does not produce Christ-centered faith, nor does his teaching speak of our heavenly Father and the Savior. The fruit of Muhammad's labor bore Islam, a world religion that undermines the heart of the Christian faith.

MUHAMMAD'S EXISTENCE QUESTIONED

The birth of Islam is a vast topic, which is being rigorously studied by historians. New details are emerging pointing to evidence that paints a wholly different picture of Islam's formation to that found within its texts. The biographies of Muhammad and the Hadith—vast volumes containing thousands of statements of Muhammad and his companions—are all being brought into question. In brief, the stories of Muhammad, the existence of Muhammad, and the history of Muhammad are also being questioned.[5] The eyewitness accounts near to the time period of Muhammad reveal a different picture to Islam's own story.

In the late seventh century (around AD 691), a religion called Islam began to emerge. In the early eighth century, a book called the Qur'an began to exist in rudimentary form,[6] taking many years to develop into what it is today. These dates are interesting because Muslims believe Islam was in motion by Muhammad's death in AD 630 and the Qur'an written down by AD 652. However, Islam seems to have emerged at least sixty years after the biographies of Muhammad say it did. What's more, some historians question whether a prophet called Muhammad ever existed and if he had anything to do with a book called the Qur'an.[7] We know a band of raiders were making their mark in Arabia by the end of the seventh century, and by the early eighth century they had conquered parts of north Africa, invading southern Spain by AD 711.[8] They were called by different names, but as time went on they became known as Muslims who followed a religion called Islam and a prophet named Muhammad. Whoever Muhammad was, or whoever founded Islam, came up with a religion that looked differently from the teaching of Christ and behaved differently from His sacrificial service to humanity. This new religion, now called Islam, does not have a Savior who gave His life as a sacrifice to give humanity life, and the fruits of its founder(s) are different from the fruit of Christ in a person's life.

Qur'an 4:171 is one of the clearest discourses of Islam that supports Islam's opposition to the gospel: "O People of the Scripture, do not commit excess in your religion or say about Allah except the truth. The Messiah, Jesus, the son of Mary, was but a messenger of Allah and His word which He directed to Mary and a soul [created at a command] from Him. So believe in Allah and His messengers. And do not say, 'Three'; desist—it is better for you. Indeed, Allah is but one God. Exalted is He above having a son. To Him belongs whatever is in the heavens and whatever is on the earth." If this was Muhammad's teaching, he really did undermine the gospel!

THERE IS NO NEED FOR MUHAMMAD

The Lord Jesus closes His Sermon on the Mount by exhorting us to build our lives on the rock! That rock was Christ, whose words we listen to and act upon (Matt. 7:24–26). Muhammad did not follow the way of Jesus. On every core point of the gospel, Muhammad, (or those he represents) taught the opposite. What's more, the Bible tells us that the Father used to speak to us through the prophets, many of whom met with God while they were alive, but today He speaks through His Son (Heb. 1:1–3). This means there is no need for the arrival of Muhammad after the finished work of Christ on the cross.

DISCUSS AND REFLECT

1. Compare and contrast Jesus and Isa.

2. What does the Qur'an say about Muhammad?

3. How do the Bible and the Qur'an differ on the topics of good deeds, treasures, and kingdoms?

4. What does the latest research say about Muhammad and the birth of Islam?

5. Biblically speaking, why is there no need for Muhammad?

PART 3

Understanding Islamic Differences

CHAPTER 10

Understanding "Traditional" Islam

The usual bright and energetic atmosphere of my Afghani family's home had taken on a somber tone. An uncle from Afghanistan was visiting, and my friend and I were ushered into the room to meet him, unusual because men and women remained in separate rooms when extended family members came to visit. But we had been a part of the family for a few years now and welcomed as siblings and daughters.

We were served food with the others, and then it came to tea and delicious Asian biscuits. We had been quiet until that point, when suddenly the Talib uncle decided to challenge Christianity by equating it with Western debauchery. Quick quiet prayers shot up from both of us, and I knew we shouldn't remain quiet as the name of Jesus was dragged through the mud. We had never conversed with a member of the Taliban before, but we trusted the prompting of the Lord and responded. As respectfully as possible, I countered what he said and mentioned Jesus's own condemnation of debauched behavior and His call for us to live holy lives. I agreed with the uncle that the West had some major issues, but didn't every country, seen and unseen? Even Afghanistan is rife with hidden sin and abuse. I didn't push it but shared a bit about Jesus and then let it rest. He was not used to anyone countering him, much less a Western woman. We had come face-to-face with historical traditional Islam.

THE TALIBAN IS A fascinating study because of its allegiance to ancient Islamic law and enactment of the life of Muhammad. They dress like Muhammad, with men wearing calf-length dresses and having henna-dyed beards, all emulating Muhammad. This is *Salafi* Islam practiced by Muslims who wish to copy Muhammad in a literal way. To them obeying Muhammad is to also obey him in dress, speech, and action.

It has always surprised me how many commentators on Islam imply today's traditional and literal forms of Islam originate from Saudi Wahhabism or the Egyptian Muslim brotherhood. Certainly, Islamic theologians from the twentieth century have greatly impacted modern-day versions of Islam, including radical[1] Islam, but they are not the source of it. That kind of Islam has always existed.

Hassan Al-Bana (d. 1949) founder of the Muslim Brotherhood and Sayyid Qutb (d. 1966) are two influential traditional leaders behind views on women and violence seen on the world stage today. Their treatises such as Sayyid's *In the Shade of the Qur'an*[2] are still available in Islamic bookstores. Writers like these are troubled by the modernization of their religion and the debauchery they see in the West. They exhort fellow Muslims to return to their texts and traditions. For them textual Islam, rooted in the life of Muhammad, is the solution. Unfortunately, it can't be found in him because his life's practice encouraged a resurgence of aggressive and, at worst, terrorist activity. Muslim friends do not usually know that the Qur'an encourages terror (Q 8:12), much less that Muhammad engaged in acts that caused terror.[3]

CITATIONS IN ISLAMIC SOURCES

Thankfully, many Muslims do not know these texts and instead follow the parts of Islamic law and examples from Muhammad's life that don't include violence. The opposing view of this can be found in the book by historian Dario Fernandez-Morera, *The Myth of the Andalusian Paradise.*[4] The author supports his thesis through multiple primary sources from many languages. I cannot highlight enough the importance of this detail.

Modern Muslim resources rarely cite the references for their claims, and yet most people, including Christians, accept their word as fact. Ed Husain's book, *The House of Islam: A Global History,*[5] is one such influential book, immensely popular among

Western politicians and academic institutions. In it he paints a romantic vision of Islamic history. But the lack of footnotes from Islamic and Qur'anic sources to support his claims is striking. Compared to *The Myth of the Andalusian Paradise*, it does not stand up to historical scrutiny. The same goes for traditional Muslims who quote Hadith, referencing only the person who said it, and the general source. For example, they might say "narrated by Aisha,"[6] in Bukhari. Bukhari is made up of multiple volumes and thousands of Hadith. I've spent may hours trawling through Hadith looking for the exact location of a supposed Hadith.[7]

CONCERNS OF TRADITIONALISTS

Traditionalists look to the Qur'an, the Traditions (i.e., the Sunna), and to Shari'ah law, compiled in the "golden era" of Islam (the first generation of Muslims). Though modernist commentators refer to some of the same sources, their interpretations and conclusions are in striking contrast.[8] One reason for this disparity can be found in the different verses and stories Muslims use to support their given opinions. Modernist Muslims are particularly picky about which Hadith they will follow. Traditionalists have good reason for not accepting modernists and the perceived "despicable" life of Westerners. Take the topic of women in Islam. Traditionalists contrast the honorable life of the Muslim woman, advocated by their holy texts, to their low view of Western women.[9] While Christians also find discomfort in modern trends, unfortunately they too are confined into the category of the "immoral Western women."[10] Muslims do not realize that there are more Christians outside the Western world than in it, and its Savior was born in the Middle East. It takes godly men and women and families living alongside, or as seen by traditional Muslims, to burst through misconceptions of Christianity.

POLES APART

Within Islam an ongoing debate is in motion between modernist and traditionalist Muslims. The roles of men and women and the topic of peace and violence are at the heart of the competing sides.

Traditionalists constantly look back to the time before Islam called "ignorance" (*jahiliyyah*) in Islamic theology. Everything is compared to this time of ignorance into which Islam emerged as a renewal of society.[11]

Much more could be said, but when most people speak about Islam, they are generally referring to the beliefs and practices of traditional Muslims. Simply put, traditional Muslims make up the majority of Muslims, and they hold to fourteen hundred years of Islamic tradition. They take their texts and

Muhammad's biography seriously, though what they know of his life is usually determined by what their religious leader (Imam) teaches. Take the Afghani family whose children learned the whole Qur'an by the age of twelve and whose practice was traditional. They saw Muhammad as a kind man, and they were kind. Yet within their own extended family, they had Taliban members who supported the Talib cause. It is as if the same family has had access to different texts and teaching, and therein lies the complexity of Islam.

DISCUSS AND REFLECT

1. When did traditional and Salafi Islam begin?

2. Do Islamic texts encourage violence in the name of Allah? How can the Christian biblically respond to this teaching?

3. What are the concerns of traditional Muslims?

4. How can Christians burst through Muslim misconceptions about them?

5. What are some of the discussions Muslims are having about their own theology?

CHAPTER 11

Understanding "Moderate" Muslims

"Christian women have only recently been liberated, but Islam has always treated women as equal to men!" Repeatedly hearing these claims drove me to dig through the Qur'an and Islamic texts. Qur'an[1] 2; 4; 33; and 65, plus its end-times verses, do not lead us to the same conclusion. I couldn't ignore the stark difference found in the Qur'an to the claims Muslims made about their "ennoblement of women."

Repeatedly, Muhammad is seen as a feminist, an ennobler of women, a protector of widows, an honorable husband. Muslim university students, Muslims in government, Muslims in cosmopolitan cities, and in books written by Muslim feminists uphold this assumption.

Every Islamic meeting and public debate on the matter had Muslims claiming equality for men and women in Islam and suppression for women in Christianity. "Islam is the solution to the West's problems!" "Muhammad ennobled women!"

MUSLIM APOLOGISTS POUR THEIR energies into articles and public statements addressing the issue. Muslim feminists write book after book reinterpreting Islamic texts on the matter. Some belittle Christian apologists who keep highlighting the matter, as if we should not, because to them it is not an issue. Their many books tell another story, and while the modern thinker may appreciate their interpretative efforts, their own texts, the Qur'an, and the life of Muhammad, oppose their arguments.[2]

Progressive Muslims and their supporters continue to reinterpret the Qur'an for a modern audience. Often pointing to perceived "archaic" practices in the Bible, then highlighting a couple of Qur'anic verses to support equality, such as Qur'an 33:35 and Qur'an 4:1, which are repeated throughout multiple treatises. In my twenties I was troubled by the number of Muslims I met who did not follow the religion written within their holy texts. It mobilized me to read the varied arguments within Islam, to read their texts as much as possible, and get to grips with the tug-of-war within Islam on the value, roles, and standing of men and women. I completed a master's thesis on women in Islam because huge numbers of the world's population have signed up to this religion, which means their lives are deeply impacted by their doctrines of God, men, and women.

What does Allah say about women, and what behavior does he teach men? What about Muslims living in the West? What does the Qur'an say about this, and can a true Muslim adapt to secular society, upholding the freedoms and liberties in the West?

"There is not moderate or immoderate Islam. There is only one Islam," claimed Turkey's former president Recep Tayyip Erdogan.[3] To him "moderate" Islam is a construction of the West to weaken Islam. He represents most Muslims, some say as much as about 75 percent of Muslims, especially in Muslim lands. When we speak of Islamic practices and beliefs, we usually mean traditional/historical Islam—fourteen hundred years of Islamic tradition. A minority of Muslims, largely living in the West or in big cities in Islamic lands, will disagree with Erdogan, calling themselves "progressive," "feminist," "moderate," "enlightened." We meet them in our schools and workplaces, and they will also be influential in secular institutions or interreligious dialogues.

So, what is a moderate, or "enlightened," Muslim?

INFLUENTIAL "PROGRESSIVE" ISLAM

Moderate Muslims usually align with left-leaning political parties in America and Europe. Muslims are often politically engaged and rise through political parties. They would not accept that Islam has historically moved to dominate all peoples in their path. They disparage those who point out historical accounts of abuse and slavery at the instigation of Islamic teaching.

They believe in the spread of Islam (similar to how Christians wish for the spread of the gospel) but are more aligned to secularism. They tend to be pluralistic in attitude and work well within secular educational facilities, which accommodate non-Christian religious voices, and are influential in Western politics. Yet their ideas are open to critique, and when put alongside Islamic texts, their views are difficult to support.

That said, some of the more radical secular pundits in Western politics fit well within the suppressive tendencies of Islamic law. Take the shutting down of free speech on many levels in the West and ponder how many Islamic leaders support it. Think about Muslim leaders who today suppress an opposing opinion, and ask if many, or any, would allow an open critique of their religious history. While pointing out atrocities, such as the transatlantic slave trade, how many admit knowledge about the pan-African, trans-Saharan Islamic slave trade, existing long before and lasting much longer than its successor.[4] How would they respond if the slavery of millions of African and European women and girls had its source in edicts of the Qur'an and the life of Islam's founder, Muhammad?[5]

These topics are too vast to unpack now,[6] but the modernization of Islam becomes complicated and untenable when Qur'anic text and Muhammad's example are accepted at face value.

ISLAM AND PROGRESS

What about the claim of the West's reliance on "Islamic invention" for its progress today? Many Muslims make such a claim, but did Islam empower progress, science, mathematics, architecture, and medical advances? Or was it Christians and Jews living among them with Arabic names, who translated texts into Arabic, to give Arab scientists and philosophers access to Western, African, and Eastern innovation? Without a shadow of a doubt, Christian Arabs were at the heart of Islamic progress—sometimes as slaves, whose expertise was utilized by their Islamic owners.[7] Non-Muslims living under Islamic law, like those who were responsible for so much of this progress, are called dhimmis, and later Mozarab (from the Arabic *mustarib*, meaning "Arabicized").[8] Muslims will say it means "protected people," but in Islamic law it works out as subjugated and second-class citizens and historically much loss of life.[9]

What has this got to do with understanding Islam? The claims and topics being discussed are at the heart of internal debates within the Muslim community and of interest to those outside Islam engaging the religion. They often come up in conversations between Muslims and Christians.

The history of Islam through the centuries—its quick advance and conquest through North and East Africa, into

Southern Europe, and then through Turkey to Western China—demands a deeper look at its texts.

THEOLOGY DEVELOPED WITH EXPANSION

Islamic texts and beliefs developed alongside the quick spread of Islam. As Islam's first warriors entered North African Christian lands and southern Spain's monasteries and churches, clear directives to deny a Savior called the Christ, His crucifixion, and the Holy Trinity, found their way into Islamic texts. As North Africa's influential Christian citadels were destroyed, or taken over, all the way to southern Spain's churches, Islamic caliphs and jurists supported these movements with text and law. The development of Islamic law coincides with this mass movement of people. The magnificent fortress of Córdoba still stands today, built with the stones from destroyed churches by Islamic slave warriors from Africa, haunted by the crucifixions of Christians on its ancient doors in ancient times.[10] Meaning the supposed "ennoblement" of Islam seen today has a sinister history, deserving of time spent on research. A history largely ignored by Western commentators, educators, and Muslims in policy. Those same policy makers demand an answer for the West's involvement in slavery and conquest, ignoring their far wider reaching and historically longer Islamic conquest and slavery by Arab and African slave drivers. Fernandez-Morera's meticulously footnoted book on the matter—*The Myth of the Andalusian Paradise*—encapsulates this history from multiple sources, Islamic and Christian.

THE SOURCE OF TRUE ENLIGHTENMENT

So, where does true enlightenment come from? From secularism? No. Our societies are destroying themselves through secularism. Through Islam? No. Islam destroyed societies in its path on and off for fourteen hundred years, this from Islam's own texts. From Christianity? Now here's an explosive answer. Yes!

Christians also engage in sinful behavior not taught in the Bible. But if a Christian abuses another, it is *not* from an edict of the Lord, contrary to some edicts of Allah. There will always be followers who do and followers who do not live out a religion's tenets, but the path to understanding a religion is by reading its texts and looking at its founder! For Muslims, that is the Qur'an and the life of Muhammad. For Christians, that is the Bible and the life of Jesus. Does the Qur'an control and suppress women and destroy men's purity, contrary to claims of "ennoblement" by Muslims? Yes (Q 2:22–223; 4:3, 34; 33:37, 53; 65:1–6). Did Muhammad abuse and hurt women. Yes. "O Prophet, indeed We have made lawful to you your wives to whom you have given their due compensation and *those your right hand possesses* from what Allah has returned to you [of captives]" (Q 33:50, emphasis added). For more on the topic of sexual slavery, see Q 4:24–25; 23:6; 24:34; 70:30.

Does the Bible control and suppress women and destroy men's purity? No (Matt. 5:28–29; 15:19–20). Did Jesus abuse and hurt women when He lived among us? No. Both the Old and New Testaments are clear about protecting the vulnerable, the widow, the orphan (including orphan girls). In Old Testament times God demanded the life of the perpetrator for a rape victim (Deut. 22:25), treatment of others above oneself (Matt. 7:12; 1 Cor. 10:24), slaves to be seen as brothers (Philem. 16), love toward both friend and foe (Luke 6:27–28), forgiveness (Eph. 4:32), and trust that He will avenge (Lev. 19:18; 1 Pet. 3:19). These edicts apply to all situations and condemn human abuse of others.

Jesus is the one through whom we become "enlightened." Both the Old and New Testaments testify to this. "The people walking in darkness have seen a great light; a light has dawned on those living in the land of darkness" (Isa. 9:2). "For my eyes have seen your salvation. You have prepared it in the presence of all peoples—a light for revelation to the Gentiles and glory to your people Israel" (Luke 2:30–32).

DISCUSS AND REFLECT

1. Give an overview of how moderate Muslims think about Islam. Does the Qur'an support their views?

2. What topics are at the heart of discussions between traditional and moderate Muslims?

3. How would you respond if a friend claimed Islam is a reason for Western progress?

4. What Bible verses can we use to respond to troubling aspects of Muhammad's life?

5. How does a person become "enlightened"?

CHAPTER 12

Understanding "Mystical" Islam

As we walked through the streets of Tehran, we were struck by the contradictory manifestations of Islam around us. Publicly we kept a watch for any "religious police" who ensured our veils covered enough of our faces—in Iran a woman cannot leave the house without a veil (hijab) on.

Our Muslim friends helped us explore Iran's beautiful cities and historical sites, introduced us to Persian beauty methods—making us unrecognizable once made up—and spoke of their unique spiritual journeys, different from the traditional forms of Islam taught by the regime.

With us they visited a church and wondered at the peace they felt when they sat in the halls of that ancient building. Yet it was their own search for peace and spiritual connection with Allah that both intrigued and concerned us.

A friend of theirs practiced Eastern meditations and participated in passing on spiritual experiences to her many Muslim clients.

A combination of Islamic love poems and religious words were said over women relaxing in their studios as incantations, prayers, and mystical practices were enacted above them. For them, this was a connection with the divine. They accessed tangible spiritual states, a feeling of happiness and calm. Yet as we witnessed their lives, this state remained fleeting.

Their art and creative writing, for which Persians are known, reflected an unsettling spiritual condition. One "spiritual friend" depicted Jesus with a black hole over half His face. For me as a Christian, it spoke of blasphemy, and the small temple with idols and candles burning in the alcove of this friend's home revealed that we were not beholding the God who loves them. It was alluring. It was also dangerous. It was unsettling. It reminded us of Hindu temples and Buddhist shrines, and it spoke of a pagan method of connecting with a power beyond them.

THIS FORM OF ISLAM is massively attractive to Western Muslims. Some refer to themselves as Sufi Muslims, others just as Muslims. Others adhere to offshoots of Islam, such as Alevism, popular among Kurdish people in Turkey, or even more distant to Islam, the Alawites of Syria.

Influential converts to Islam from Western nations who teach in our universities and influence our governments often adhere to mystical forms of Islam.[1] Islam's history is reinterpreted through a romantic grid and remains attractive to modern

Muslims, in part due to their belief that historically Sufis have been peaceful. This myth does not accurately reflect the harsh reality of the rise of Sufism through the Middle Ages, and much like other ancient Islamic movements, violence is a part of their story.

Mystical religious elements from Arabia and Asia, alongside Syriac Christian hymns, were adapted into Islam and emphasized by Sufi forms of Islam. Islam's view of angels and jinn (demons) and core pagan practices still present in many Muslim lives point to its mystical heart. Even the once-in-a-lifetime Muslim pilgrimage to Mecca reflects ancient pagan origins.

This spiritual form of Islam integrates well into secular visions of spirituality, and followers from both traditions need not compromise the precepts of their lives. Being spiritual is favorable in Western pluralistic societies, as it is a fluid form of religion, based on heart connection or spiritual experiences. It fits well with a rejection of formalized religion.

SPIRITUALITY THAT LEADS AWAY FROM GOD

The Bible highlights spiritualism throughout its pages. It repeatedly shows how the Lord works to rid us of a spirituality that ultimately leads us away from Him. Mystical Islam may not appear as imposing as traditional Islam, but if it is not from our heavenly Father, then it is worth a biblical response, especially as it becomes more prominent in fluctuating modern society.

Since I began studying Islam, I have set out to read Islamic theology directly from Muslims. I wanted to know what *they* believed. It has helped me understand the different interpretations of the Islamic religion and to better understand my Muslim friends and the changing trends within Islam.

Sufi Muslim author, A. Helwa, has written a book, *Secrets of Divine Love: A Spiritual Journey into the Heart of Islam*, which seeks to connect with those searching for a "deeper intimacy" and "loving relationship"' with Allah. Its descriptions fit right into the self-help and well-being sections of large bookstores, filled with books aiding readers to find their spiritual potential, true meaning, and purpose for life. She draws upon "spiritual secrets of the Qur'an," mystical poems, and stories from Islamic prophets and spiritual masters. The book wants to reignite people's faith and deepen their connection with Allah.

The aim of the book, and of many other mystical writers, draws us in, just like a good Christian book would. It responds to some of our heart's deepest questions and yearnings—intimacy with God. It claims to be a guiding light. Truth and understanding. This form of Islam seeks to access deeper spiritual truths through the words of the Qur'an, to find a deeper connection to Allah.

This mysticism is found in most Islamic interpretations and practices. The recitation of the Qur'an at Friday prayers in mosques, weddings, funerals, and gatherings ignites a powerful spiritual response in Muslims. Power is seen and experienced when the congregation gathers to hear Islamic prayers and readings. For many Shi'ah Muslims—references to Islamic poets such as the renowned Rumi, known to focus on "divine love," appeals to the heart needs of the modern world.

SPIRITUAL BUT NOT OF CHRIST

The book makes biblical claims such as the love of God, being created with a purpose, death as the beginning of life, being made for more than dying and going to heaven, and drawing closer to God. Yet there are some giveaways to its non-Christian and secular foundations, such as being able to master our own egos, repentance that works and changes sin into good, and God as transcendent. But more importantly, the god it leads the reader to is *not* our Creator. It is not the Trinity. Jesus is nowhere to be seen. God's suffering to rescue us from our egos and sin is removed. There is no loving heavenly Father. The empowering Holy Spirit is not at the heart of transformation. The aims of the book speak to some Christian aims, but the god it proclaims leads to paganism.

Mystical Sufi friends may hold to some similar ideals about God, which at first glance sound like the Lord, but ultimately Sufiism leads them away from Him. That means our talking point with them, and any Muslim, is always Christ. Mystical religions do not have Christ. And He is the way to our heavenly Father and true life in eternity. Conversations about the Lord Jesus will always point out the differences between any Islamic interpretation and Christianity.

Conversations about the Lord Jesus will always point out the differences between any Islamic interpretation and Christianity.

POSITIVE AND NEGATIVE RESPONSES

Our mystically minded Muslim friends need Christ as much as we do. At times they need deliverance if they have dabbled in the occult, knowingly or unknowingly. The Lord Jesus exemplified in His life what to do in such situations (Matt. 8:16; 9:25; Luke 4:41; 8:29). They will either respond with a desire to know Jesus more, harden their hearts and turn away, or worse, turn to hate. I recall a time when a mystically minded Muslim friend longed to hear more, asked for prayer, and asked me to read the Bible to her as she fought battles with demonic powers. On another occasion my standing on Jesus, rejection of combining Islam and Christianity, resulted in a Twitter attack against me from a well-known political Sufi Muslim.

The results of our engagement are not up to us; we are simply called to hold to biblical truth about God and love our Muslim neighbor, staying true to Christ's Great Commission. It might mean a challenge against an Islamic belief, even if it seems close to Christian ideals, or a prayer for a Muslim's felt needs, but if the Great Commission of Christ remains central to our message, then we will remain clear on how to understand and respond to both the religion of Islam and its people with their multiple interpretations.

DEMONS FLEE

It is alarming how many missionaries living among Muslim families have had to contend with demonic forces haunting their Muslim friends. On a spring evening in California, my friend and I watched our Muslim friends cover every opening in the room where we were all about to sleep. The front door, our door, and the windows had towels and pillows placed over them. When we asked about it, we learned it was to keep us safe from the *jinn* (spirit beings who can be evil), as in demons. We told them that two Christians were with them and there was no need to fear—the demons would not bother them that night.

The stories of Jesus give us clarity on how to deal with such situations. When Jesus was confronted directly by the devil (Matt. 4:1–11), he quoted Scripture to confront Satan's clever lies. The situation must have been distressing—a satanic presence is an ugly experience—yet Jesus had to face the devil in person and hear his lies. Lies close to truth yet far from truth, playing on common temptations we face—grandeur, power, submission to false gods.

If an ideology denies the risen Lord Jesus as our Savior, then that ideology has not come from God (hence demonic harassment), and therefore we can be honest about this with our Muslim friends but absolutely give them the solution. I usually pray clearly in the name of Jesus and explain why before I do. Yet we cannot cast a demon out if our friends do not accept Christ (Matt. 12:43–45). We must become storytellers about Jesus to see lives changed, especially as the different forms of Islam include practices which allow malign jinn into their lives.

DISCUSS AND REFLECT

1. Why is Sufi Islam popular in the West?

2. What are core Sufi views of spirituality?

3. How do we theologically respond to mystical Islam?

4. What Bible verses encourage you, especially when saddened by Muslim friends rejecting the Savior?

5. How do we biblically respond to demonic presence that might appear in some Islamic homes?

PART 4

Understanding Migration and Mission

CHAPTER 13

Islamic Migration and Mission

"You are afraid of what we will do to you when Britain becomes Islamic!" snarled a key Muslim missionary to London. It was a normal Sunday afternoon for our team of evangelists who met weekly to pray and prepare after church to head out to Speakers' Corner.

Speakers' Corner has a long history of free speech in the UK, initially as the platform below Marble Arch where those condemned to death could say their last words. Once the death penalty by hanging was removed, then it became a place for politicians to practice their speeches to the crowds before going to parliament. More recently it has become a hub for Islamic mission. Muslim missionaries have ruled Speakers' Corner for decades, and today it is their custom to film unsuspecting tourists as they grill them about their religious or nonreligious views. It is then posted online to become fodder for Islamic mockery—if the comments section is to be believed.

That Sunday afternoon I had held up the biography of Muhammad. I was asking if Asma the poetess, who had written

Qur'anic verse against Muhammad, should have been killed for doing so.[1] Or if the fate of some of the teenage girls, whose husbands Muhammad's men had just killed, should be married off and distributed to him and his men. A Muslim woman had been discussing women's roles within Islam with me and wanted to converse more. She had to tell the men to stop trying to break up our conversation and let us speak with each other. She had never read these stories out of the biographies of Muhammad or the verses relating to similar scenarios in the Qur'an.

We were not speaking with Muslim friends; we were speaking with Muslims who believed the actions of Muhammad were right and good, even when it meant agreeing with the death of an innocent mother who wrote poetry or of widowed teenagers being given by Muhammad to his men. A nasty question on the topic was leveled at me, which I won't mention here, but I knew I had seen the underbelly of a religion that would not bring protection and harmony to non-Muslim women if it were ever to become dominant in the land.

HIGHLIGHTING SUCH EVENTS IS difficult. Sharing a tough image of Islam is hard. Yet these difficult facts are supported by reams of Islamic texts. I love my Muslim friends, and at times it means tough questions and critiques need to be made about the religion they have committed their lives to. But having to challenge those we love can pull at our heartstrings. It makes us wonder how

God must feel when He confronts us with our false ideas about Him and sin issues when we stray from biblical truth.

That said, we need to think a bit about the growth of Islam in Western lands and consider what Islamic texts teach.

DOCTRINE OF MIGRATION IN ISLAM

A doctrine of Islamic migration is found within Islamic law. In part it is based on the migration of Muhammad (called *Al Hijrah*[2]). It refers to Muhammad's migration from Mecca to Medina in Arabia in the early seventh century, where he was supposed to have lived. Muslims claim he was initially persecuted but then went on to conquer Medina and Mecca, after which many began to follow Islam (Q 59:8–9). Romantic revisions of the history celebrate this event while ignoring the force behind Islamic conversions and exile of people from their lands. Other historians question whether these stories have any evidence outside of Islamic sources, and the history or even existence of Muhammad is in question. Yet for the average Muslim, his story is deeply significant for them, as he is an example for them (Q 33:21).

Muslim leaders in the West often scoff at those who raise this point that Al Hijra is still relevant for today's context. They state it is no longer valid or applicable to modern society. On one level they are right. However, it is still a part of Islamic law, based on the life of Muhammad, and encouraged by edicts of the Qur'an (Q 9 and 59 specifically speak of migration and exile). The theology of migration may not be overtly taught in every Islamic community, but it is practiced overtly or unknowingly and alluded to in multiple Qur'anic verses, "Those who believe, and have left their homes and striven with their wealth and their lives in Allah's way are of much greater worth in Allah's sight. These are they who are triumphant" (Q 9:20; 9:41).[3]

Many secular commentators focus on the growth of Islam. Some welcome Muslims with open arms, while others reject them and foster hate. Still others incite fear. Biblical Christianity takes another road.

DISTINGUISHING BETWEEN PEOPLE AND THEIR RELIGION

The way we biblically respond to Islam is different from the way we biblically respond to Muslims. As Christians we have a way of responding to people that many in the world do not understand because our way of engagement with others is the way of Christ. If we believe that "while we were still sinners, Christ died for us" (Rom. 5:8), then we too can look at someone outside of our faith, our tradition, even those holding opposing ideals and know that Christ died for them, too. They may even be antagonistic to our faith, but Christ died for them. No Muslim or secularist has such a profound grid through which to see others. It means that when Muslims migrate to our lands, we know God has brought them to us to hear the gospel, often for the first time.

Making a distinction between the people and their religion will balance our response to Islam and the movement of its people, Muslims.

The world has always had people movements. It started with Adam and Eve! And our great earthly father, Abraham, was a migrant. The statistics of migrating or displaced people around the world today are alarming. The twenty-first century has not fostered a world that encourages stability, and our world's populations are witnessing a great shift.

With the migration of Muslim people around the world, we see the *religion* of Islam on the move. Whole societies have been changed and become Islamic when Islam has taken root—either by conquering villages, towns, and nations in its path or by mass migration. North Africa is but one example, as are central Asian and Eastern nations. Whole towns in parts of Europe and communities in parts of America are deeply Islamic. We cannot be naïve about Islamic immigration. To understand it in theological terms is helpful as we engage the communities of Islam.

ISLAMIC MISSION AND LIVING UNDER ISLAM

With the migration of Muslims comes the concept of Islamic mission. Muslims are called to engage in *dawah*, which means to invite non-Muslims to Islam. All sorts of laws are provided in Islamic law to help Muslims know how to fulfil their obligations. However, while Muslims wish for the Islamization of peoples, Islamic missions is not about salvation. Salvation is uniquely a Christian teaching.

Islamic mission has historically been about dominance: to make Islam the ruler of nations, much like secularism seeks to do today. Great efforts have been made in Western society to secularize our institutions and politics. It is as if religion had no place in public spheres of life. It means the silencing and sidelining of Christians. This is how Islam has historically worked.

In Islam, Christians would be called *ahl ul-dhimmah* or *dhimmis*, those who submit (willingly, or usually unwillingly) to Islamic rule. Modern Muslims like to claim it was a protection for Christians and Jews who abided by *dhimmi* rules, but in reality it was a way to keep (literally) one's head attached to one's shoulders! It was some sort of protection from the extremes of living under Islamic slavery. In essence, dhimmis are non-Muslims who are forced to live as second-class citizens under Islamic governance.[4] Some Muslims today reject this teaching found in Islamic law; nevertheless their texts have informed scores of generations of Muslims, and for many today the laws remain authoritative.

In the Sunni Hanbali law, we read the following: "They [dhimmis] cannot ride a horse. Nor have centre stage at events.

They are not to be greeted with peace. Dhimmis are forbidden to build churches. Their houses cannot be taller than Muslim homes. Their religion must be hidden away, and not made public."⁵ This was implemented in North Africa and then in Islamic Spain during its four-hundred-year occupation.

Muslims who accept this history usually say the skirmishes of the early Muslims were a defensive response against outside aggressors. Moderate Muslims may disagree that Islam was about gaining territory and power. Dominance to them is not Islamic but the result of misguided outside influences. Moderate Muslims seek a pluralistic, attractive interpretation of this same history, making it suitable for the secular mind.

Yet Islam's texts speak for themselves. You do not have to dig far to read of the example lived out by Muhammad as he waged war on Jewish and Christian communities. Qur'an 9 is a key chapter on this, as are the details found in Alfred Guillaume's translation of the earliest biography of Muhammad.

Islam has been a sociopolitical movement since it began, meaning it is about gaining territory. It has always had a political edge to it, impacting people politically and socially, often more than spiritually. Thankfully, most of our Muslim friends have little knowledge of the Islamic ideals just outlined, or if they do, they reject them and live their lives peaceably alongside Christian friends. This is where religion is often different from its people.

And this is where Christians respond to Muslims differently than they do to Islam.

When we consider this fact, we need to understand God's mission and God's response to migrating Muslims. Some have come by choice—the immigrant; others by force—the refugee. We are called to care for neighbors, known or new, and provide a solution to the struggles they have, and that solution starts with Jesus.

DISCUSS AND REFLECT

1. What is the Islamic doctrine of *Al Hijrah*?

2. What Qur'anic verse supports it, and where else is it found in Islamic texts?

3. Why is it important to respond to Islam differently to how we respond to Muslims?

4. Who are dhimmis, and how are they treated in Islamic law?

5. What is God's response to people movements?

CHAPTER 14

Biblical Migration and Mission

Serving at the Turkish-speaking church called Care (Çare in Turkish) was an honor. A beautiful word in English, spelled the same in Turkish, meaning "help" or "remedy." Those first years in mission set a standard for witness among peoples who hail from Islamic lands.

Our church leaders were loving and sacrificial in action yet firm and clear in their communication of Christ. They understood Islam and had lived in Islamic lands. Some of our leaders had been migrants to Islamic lands and then expelled from those countries for sharing about Jesus and seeing Muslims come to Christ.

Upon their arrival into the UK, also came the arrival of hundreds of thousands of refugees from Turkey and Iran. Refugees were sleeping on church and mosque floors, city hostels, and crammed into hotels. Rather than give up their passion for sharing their faith with Muslims, the newly exiled missionaries sat alongside them, listened to their stories, wept with them as they wept, helped them practically, and shared the "hope within them," leading to some new migrants leaving Islam to follow Jesus.

AT THAT JUNCTURE, THE exiled missionaries from Turkey and Iran had seen people in need. They saw what the religion of those people had done to them, but they saw *behind* the religion—people who needed to hear the gospel and receive its healing balm. They ministered to both felt and spiritual needs. They understood the gravity of the migrant situation. Much as the Western world grapples with it today, thirty years later.

We are called to understand and undertake God's mission. To see people saved, which is to witness societies transformed. That's the two-step process. The transformation we speak of is not like that resulting from Islamic migration—*Al Hijra*; rather it means lives uplifted and communities positively impacted, even if initially torn apart through conversion.

ISLAM ON THE MOVE IS A NONISSUE *IF . . .*

Islam on the move is a nonissue if the church stays true to its own text and King. God has called us to stand firm (Eph. 6:13), to be salt and light (Matt. 5:13–16), and to explain the faith, even in the context of threat (2 Pet. 3:14–15). We are called to biblically respond to human ideologies: "For the weapons of our warfare *are* not carnal but mighty in God for pulling down strongholds, casting down arguments and every high thing that exalts itself against the knowledge of God" (2 Cor. 10:4–5 NKJV).

CHRISTIANS ARE BIBLICAL IMMIGRANTS

The Bible calls Christians to migrate! But what is biblical migration? Well, if it is like Abraham—our forefather—then it is to leave country and town and go toward another land. If it is like Moses, it is to walk out of slavery and embark on an adventure with God and His people to follow Him to freedom, the promised land. Or if it is like the apostle Paul, it is to leave the comfort of home, rent a house, and witness to anyone who knocks on the door (Acts 28:30–31).

Biblical migration is about following the Lord, inviting all people to follow Him, so together we can find freedom. It is not about dominance; it is about rescue. It is about friendship with Jesus. It might mean migrating out of our front door to welcome a new neighbor who comes from another land, or it might mean a painful plane trip flying over the Atlantic Ocean to ministry yet unknown, to people little understood. Either way, it is a wonderful call and one which can see communities and whole societies transformed through life with Jesus.

When we see through God's eyes, we don't see "a religion"; we see "a person." Christ did not die for Islam. He died for Muslims.

When we see through God's eyes, we don't see "a religion"; we see "a person."

Jesus's sermon on the Mount outlines three types of people we might meet outside our homes—neighbors, enemies, and persecutors. And He tells the church to "love your neighbor," "love your enemy," and "pray for your persecutors." He tells us not to curse and to be peacemakers (Rom. 12:14; Heb. 12:14).

WITNESSING WHEN FREEDOMS ARE REMOVED

We are able to biblically stand firm and defend the faith, even in a world where freedoms are diminishing by imposing ideologies like atheism and Islam. We can do this when God is first in our hearts! "Sanctify the Lord God in your hearts, and always be ready to give a defense" (1 Pet. 3:15 NKJV).

This verse became especially poignant when we traveled through countries like Turkey, Tajikistan, and Iran. In none of these countries were we free to proclaim Christ, not without pushback from authorities or communities steeped in Islam. In Turkey we visited a family under twenty-four-hour "protection," though it was in part also surveillance, due to threats from the local mosque. They must have been doing something right to receive such threats!

In Central Asia we focused on aid work and prayed we'd be able to share with those we met. I often wondered how we could share Christ if we stayed long term, likely through serving in the church and praying for God to open doors.

In Iran we carried a Bible in Persian and asked the Lord for the right person to give it to, and that wonderful moment came on a seven-hour coach trip through Iran. A veiled lady quietly slipped it beneath her hijab to read later, and while we didn't speak loudly on Christian issues, as too many eyeballs were looking our way at the strange spectacle of a Western woman deep in conversation with a fully veiled Iranian, we were able to share a few thoughts with each other. She now has the Word of God to read, and that can minister to her profoundly.

The Lord guides His people to where there are opportunities to speak for Him, not just to share faith but to encourage isolated Christians. In one Islamic country, we arrived at our friend's house at 2:00 a.m. after a long journey through the desert, and our new host burst out with joy, "You are Christians!" as she opened the door. We hurried in and in quieter tones spoke of our shared faith. What a joy to speak with her and find a sister in the heart of a Muslim land. She had quietly come to faith ten years earlier, just by hearing the truth.

In the hills of Turkey, another lady welcomed us into her home. When she heard we were Christians, as we were always open about our faith, she shared with us her own love of the local ancient Armenian church in town. She was an abandoned woman; her husband had walked out on her. She, however, had received a New Testament at a historical orthodox church while traveling. With joy we spoke about our shared faith, hers found through reading the Scriptures.

The testimonies all point to how an environment closed to God's ways does not mean an environment closed to gospel proclamation. God will always provide a way. The Lord gives us wisdom and strength in seemingly hopeless circumstances. This is why starting with Christ, rather than cultural human restrictions, opens the doors for gospel sharing, "For God has not given us a spirit of fear, but one of power, love, and sound judgment. So don't be ashamed of the testimony about our Lord, or of me his prisoner. Instead, share in suffering for the gospel, relying on the power of God" (2 Tim. 1:7–8 NKJV). He goes on to exhort us to share in suffering for the gospel, relying on the power of God. "He has saved us and called us with a holy calling" (1 Tim. 1:9 NKJV). This is from a man who often found himself in prison and having to defend his faith before the authorities!

Doing a Bible study on the topic of sharing the faith in all circumstances is a deeply convicting and fascinating exercise.[1] God's mission field is all around us, and when we join Him, our own lives and those around us are transformed. While it may be scary to witness the lack of wisdom in some of our government immigration policies, when lives are turned around for Christ, people movements no longer seem so threatening. Right on our doorstep we could see the name of the Father, the Son, and the Holy Spirit proclaimed on the lips of millions of Muslims—if we follow in the footsteps of Christ. I recall the words of a ten-year-old refugee to the UK who was a part of Çare Church, "They can take my life, but they can't take Jesus from me!" May Christ be exalted as His people move into lands, seeking to love their neighbors with His love. May Christ be exalted as people living in Islam-held lands come to know Him and serve Him. May Christ be exalted as people move into our lands, and we have the opportunity to share the gospel with them.

DISCUSS AND REFLECT

1. What verses help us know how to respond to Islam growing worldwide?

2. What does it mean to be "a biblical immigrant"?

3. What can we be sure of when our freedoms are removed?

4. Has there been a time in your life when the Lord opened a door to witness that human beings had shut?

5. People may try take our lives from us, but what can they never take?

CHAPTER 15

Biblically Responding to Islam

A British convert to Islam stood on his stepladder at London's famous Speakers' Corner. In this historic place of free speech, he, along with the many Muslim missionaries, engage non-Muslims (primarily Christians) in debates about religion. Christian attitudes of charity, listening, and caring for those he disagreed with were absent, and his speeches were peppered with disinformation about Christians and Christianity.

I stood at the back of a fast-growing crowd listening to public insults against our Lord and Savior, praying fervently that at least one person in the crowd who was a Christian would step forward and defend the faith. Preferably a man, since the crowd was packed with men, nodding in agreement or standing with gleeful smiles at the humiliation of Christians. "Please, heavenly Father, give courage to a Christian to speak up and defend Your name."

The barrage of insults continued against the way of Christ: "Christianity is to blame for the depravity on our streets! Christianity is to blame for the materialism driving our city!"

Suddenly righteous indignation and annoyance—not the godliest response perhaps—got the better of me, and the prompting of the Holy Spirit could no longer be ignored.

Out came a squeak of objection. A mass of male eyes turned toward the high-pitched squeak that had unfortunately come from me.

On and on the Muslim missionary shouted: "Christianity is the source of our problems; it is to blame for materialism in the West!" Another throat-constricted response squeaked out, "Not true! Jesus teaches the opposite!" The eyes of Sauron, or so it seemed, shifted toward me. Rage filled Sauron's eyes. How dare a girl undermine his platform of pride, power, and, thus far, successful destruction of Christianity. Although it was not Christianity he was confronting— sin yes, and perhaps some sinful Christians, but not Christianity itself.

Trembling, heart-pounding, but needing to speak louder to be heard, I began to speak: "Jesus tells us it is easier for a camel to enter heaven than for a rich man, a rich man to enter a needle, a camel to go into a needle, than a camel into heaven, I mean a camel, a rich man to enter heaven!"

Bother it! Body shaking, voice trembling, "Jesus does not teach materialism!"

THANKFULLY THE SQUEAK DISAPPEARED, and though still shaking, we managed to have a reasonable interaction, with the Muslim missionary stepping down from his high ladder, no longer publicly attacking the Christian faith, at least for a few hours.

The Lord Jesus holds Christians to a high standard of character and actions. Our words must speak truth. Our witness is driven by love, and with time our fear will dissipate as that love grows. Love often commands a response from us, even when the situation seems hostile.

"Love the Lord your God with all your heart, with all your soul, and with all your mind. This is the greatest and most important command. The second is like it: Love your neighbor as yourself. All the Law and the Prophets depend on these two commands" (Matt. 22:37–40).

This is a profound command. It is uniquely biblical. It transforms normative human attitudes and behavior, and it sets the foundation for how Christians engage other people and their ideas. It heals. It dispels aggression. It brings people together. The command tells us how to respond to Muslims. It is not, however, how we should respond to Islam.

LOVE BUT DISAGREE

Jesus commands us to love others, but He does not tell us to love our neighbor's *ideas*. He does not encourage us to accommodate our neighbor's ways and attitudes. He does not say we should respect our neighbor's Islamic religion, or their atheism or their New Age beliefs, and all that goes along with those worldviews. Love does the opposite. To love a person means to love enough to disagree with their false ideas.

Biblical love requires a resolute and clear response, one that challenges the beliefs of people like Muhammad and British converts! Whoever founded Islam robbed a quarter of the world's population from knowing and living with the world's Savior, and God does not take kindly to ideologies that lead people away from Him.

ATTRACTION OF ISLAM

Perhaps this is where some in Christian missions have allowed compromise. Muslims often hail from ancient hospitable cultures. Missionaries can find themselves making friends more easily among Muslims than fellow Christians. Mosques can be more welcoming than churches, and a notable beauty and mysticism of dress, code of conduct, food, spices, and aromas become deeply alluring. But this is not Islam. This is ancient, often pre-Islamic culture and includes ancient cultures whose foundations were Christian.

We can appreciate the depth of culture of other religious devotees yet remain clear on our religious differences. It is loving to point out those differences because the differences between our religions forge the way to deep conversations about God and salvation.

LOVE AT THE HEART OF GOD'S LAW

Has it ever struck you how profound is Jesus's statement of how the law and words of biblical prophets hang on the two greatest commandments: love God and love one another? These are commandments taught in both the Old and New Testaments (Deut. 6:5; 10:12, 19; Lev. 19:18; Matt. 22:26–40). It means the Christian's life and witness start with loving God, the Trinity. Love this God, and you can't help but love all of creation. This God sent His Son to die for us, then the Holy Spirit to dwell with us, to guide us into a deep relationship with and knowledge of God. We can then understand the world, human beings, sin, salvation, and eternity. From there we can be clear about how we engage other religious views and how we respond to human beings who believe ideologies that undermine this living God and His way.

LOVE THOSE WHO HATE

How do we love aggressive Muslim missionaries who publicly lie about Christianity and who seem to succeed in swaying huge crowds of people away from truth? On one level the Lord despises falsehood. He hates lies and so should we. Yet God still died for that liar!

When we come across liars against the Christian faith, it can be helpful to remember how we could be just like them if we did not have allegiance to the One who transforms our hearts. It certainly held me in good stead at my first squeaky outburst against a liar. The squeaks are nothing to be proud of, funny looking back, petrifying while it happened, providing all sorts of mocking fodder to those who hate Christians. Yet our heavenly Father's love for all people compels us. The good news of Jesus compels us. The dispelling of lies compels us. In Christ we can emphatically challenge a Muslim missionary lying about Christianity, albeit squeakily! And, though we may fear and tremble, especially at our first attempt at sticking our head above the parapet, our demeanor can still manifest God's Spirit (Gal. 5:22–23). Even when we have to shout out the truth to be heard above a cacophony of noise, we can still speak in a godly manner.

After the Muslim missionary stepped down from his high ladder, I finally managed to get the camels, needles, heaven, and rich men in the right order, while praying fervently for help, as a hundred pairs of eyes turned toward us! His words continued to belittle and sting, at which point two Muslim men stepped forward, asking him why he was being so rude and stating that I, as a Christian girl, had a right to respond to his claims. And there began my first conversation with a Muslim missionary to the West. After many more years and many more conversations with Muslim missionaries and refugees from almost every Muslim land, the trembling has, by and large, disappeared, and fear no longer controls. Love now stands in its place. To put it bluntly, we hate the Muslim missionary's rhetoric, but we can love the person behind it. And that is a uniquely biblical position. It is a foundation by which societies can be transformed because it is the way of our heavenly Father (John 3:16–17), who sent His Son Jesus to take on their punishment, and if they surrender to Him, the Holy Spirit will dwell in them.

LISTEN TO THE HOLY SPIRIT

I remember when a towering and aggressive, long-robed Muslim missionary to the West towered over my five-foot Christian colleague. A few of us tried to wade through the crowd of mostly Muslim men to stand near for support and in prayer.

The Trinity was the topic of the day, and the Muslim missionary began raging about how angry the concept of the Trinity made him. "How could she believe in a Father and Son, as God!" Followed by expletives we need not mention, he kept taunting her about being filled with the Holy Spirit, interspersed with more obscenities. He mockingly claimed she should know everything if God lived inside her, and "How did God live within her?" By this time the crowd was heaving, and he had a captive audience. His rage, exaggerated to dramatic effect for his eager listeners, was in part jest as he shouted at her, "Oh! This makes me angry!" Quietly, and with a bright smile, she looked up saying, "The Holy Spirit can help you with your anger."

Chuckles murmured through the crowd as that gentle word forced his excessive and exaggerated wrath to melt away. Amused, the crowd turned their eyes on the raging bull standing before a smiling God-filled woman. His rage had lost its place, and along with the crowd he couldn't help but let a smile cover his mocking mouth.

The power of the Holy Spirit had cut through to the minds of the crowd. It had confronted the theology of Islam's god. It had defused the mockery of an angry man.

The five-foot Christian facing the towering giant of a Muslim missionary had held true to her love for her heavenly Father and His Son, our Savior. She knew the Holy Spirit was her helper. She had not budged in her explanation of this to the man in front of her. She had trusted, in those moments of hostility toward her, that the Holy Spirit would help and inspire her speech and attitude. She did not accommodate Islamic thinking on any level, even under threat, but she did know she was speaking with a human being who was made in the image of God (not in his attitude, obviously, but in his core being). Truth, along with the power of the Holy Spirit, broke through falsehood that day. Her fear of the Lord was the beginning of a wise engagement of Islam (Prov. 9:10).

DISCUSS AND REFLECT

1. What is uniquely biblical in our responses to people?

2. How are we to respond to religions that undermine Christ?

3. Why are some Christians attracted to Islam?

4. What forges the way to deep conversations about the gospel?

5. What breaks through falsehood?

PART 5

Understanding Theological Differences

CHAPTER 16

God

Standing on a conference platform, a missionary from America, working with a European mission agency, proclaimed: "Muslims just need to worship Jesus as Lord and Savior!" He believed we didn't need to bring converts into the church; they could remain in the mosque. When asked if the Muslims he had described as converts from Islam understood what Lord and Savior meant, he admitted that perhaps only 10 percent fully grasped that Jesus is God.

All had been described to American and European churches as "converts" or "Christians." Yet most were not believers, not according to God's definitions. Words were used which sounded like orthodox Christianity, but meanings of those words remained empty, and a pseudo-Christianity steeped in Islam began to emerge among Muslim communities influenced by this approach to mission.

ON ONE LEVEL FINDING similarities or leaving Muslim "converts" within Islam might seem to make our witness easier. Yet does it? Surely it leads to confusion and compromise. Most worryingly, it opens the door to heresy!

As in all relationships, God does not want a lukewarm commitment from us (Isa. 29:13; Rev. 3:15–16). We either clearly proclaim who He is, or we compromise. We belong to Him or we don't. If our theology is watered down or considered to be of the same origin as Islam, then our message about God is fickle, introducing a changeable being we cannot trust. If the community we have allegiance to is not of Him, such as a mosque, then we align ourselves with a group that is not grounded on truth.

To remain consistent and clear in our confused world means that we cannot align our faith with a religion that opposes the Trinity, Jesus, and biblical teaching about God, human beings, sin, salvation, and eternity. These key topics make for great conversations with Muslims! And so we are going to unpack them in the chapters ahead.

FOCUS ON OUR DIFFERENCES

Our theological differences open the door to deep Bible-driven spiritual experiences. The world is full of people of world religions having spiritual experiences, but meeting the living God is different. When biblical truth is at the heart of a spiritual experience, God's peace that surpasses understanding is present, and Jesus draws near.

Centering our discussions and prayers on how different God is from Allah, the Bible is from the Qur'an, and Islamic life is from biblical life profoundly aids our conversations. As does Christ's love shining through us! And it is easy to learn those differences because we have access to both the Bible and the Qur'an. We let the texts speak for themselves.

When Islamic missionaries train Muslims on how to confront Christianity, they focus on three areas:

1. The Trinity
2. The divinity of Jesus
3. The Bible

Wonderful topics to talk about, and many books have been written, especially on the reliability of the Bible and the divinity of Jesus.[1] They can be helpful to peruse, as Muslims are often taught that Christians made up the divinity of Jesus in the early fourth century at the Council of Nicaea. That early Christian conference is seen as the moment the Bible was put together and the Trinity was introduced. History itself challenges such an idea, but it permeates many Muslims' misconceptions about the Christian faith.

FIVE FOUNDATIONAL TOPICS

We will consider Islam through five foundational biblical topics:

1. God
2. Humanity
3. Sin
4. Salvation
5. Eternity

Through these subjects we can see how theologically different Islam is to the Bible.

We'll start with the biblical and Islamic views of God, considering God's name, character, and actions. Then the differing views of human beings, looking at being made in God's image, in contrast to Allah's separation from humans. Allah is "inimitable," a favorite word used by Muslim missionaries to describe how distant Allah is from creation. Next up are our contrasting views of sin. Sin either resulted in a broken relationship with God and the Son of God giving up His life in a rescue mission to save us, or sin is not the ultimate problem and continues even into eternity. To the biblical thinker, Muslims are not rescued from their sin, as Islam's paradise promotes sinful behavior. We next need to understand different views of salvation, with the Bible focused on rescuing human beings into a new sin-free life, in contrast to Islam where Allah has never embarked on a rescue mission. Culminating our study with a different view of eternity—Jesus living with His bride versus sin continuing in the Islamic paradise and the jarring thought that for Muslims, God will never live with His people.

As we consider these five areas of theological differences, it becomes clear how on every point of the gospel that Islam teaches the opposite.

WHO IS GOD? WHO IS ALLAH?

As a starting point, we will ask a few key questions about these same names and ask *who* God is. What is His name? How does He act? We also need to ask *who* Allah is.

Let's consider a few quick observations from the Qur'an, which we'll continually compare with the Lord of the biblical Scriptures. Islamic theology can become philosophical and complicated, but to simplify it, we can start with a Qur'anic verse which sums up our differences: "Say, 'He is Allah, [who is] One, . . . He neither begets nor is born, Nor is there to Him any equivalent'" (Q 112:1–4). These verses supports the Islamic doctrine of *tawhid*, a central doctrinal statement about Allah. It refers to Allah's "oneness," meaning Allah is a singular, indivisible being.

Many of the Qur'anic edicts about who God is directly challenge the biblical God. The Qur'an is concerned its readers reject the Lord Jesus as God. See how Qur'an 112 denies God could be born. It never introduces God as a Father. Though the Qur'an does allude to Isa as the spirit in Qur'an 4:171, which is sometimes translated as a soul.

Muslims often believe that the Christian view of Jesus is the result of an immoral sexual partnership between God and a human. Their dislike of Jesus's divinity arises from a negative preoccupation with His physical birth and human form. This is an Islamic problem, not a biblical one. We know from the Bible that God comes down to us (Exod. 3:14–15; Num. 8:12; John 1:1–14; Col. 1:15; Heb. 2:14), but in Islam, Allah has no form and never comes in flesh. And yet the Qur'an alludes to some descriptive parts of his appearance (Q 68:42). While debates over the matter have existed among Islamic theologians over the centuries, modern Islam does not support Allah having form, especially like us.

ALLAH IS *"ONE"*

Unlike Allah, we know God is not a one-dimensional being—our Father can give (beget[2]) His Son (John 3:16). He is one God (Deut. 6:4) made up of three Persons. That said, it is usually more helpful to stick to biblical ways of describing God (rather than theological terms like three Persons and one God) when in discussion with Muslims. His Son can take on our flesh (Phil. 2), even die on a cross (Rom. 5:8), and together, they then send us the Holy Spirit to help us know Him better and live our lives for Him (John 14–16). God's descriptions also relate to His character. If we were to sum up God to a Muslim, our God is profoundly relational, and His names and actions reflect this.

Unlike Allah, God is not a singular *one*. Allah could not take on flesh and walk with us because to become embodied would require that he abdicate any other responsibility. Heaven wasn't empty when Jesus took on flesh, and because of God's triune nature, Jesus could die, and the Spirit could raise Him again. By contrast, the universe would spiral out of control if Allah died because there would be no one to sustain it. God being three Persons enables Him to act profoundly and personally throughout our world.

The death of God's Son is an important theology that no other religion testifies to (John 3:16; Rom. 5:8). Yet this death is at the core of our faith. It is a great wonder to think on, and a powerful thought to contemplate what God must think about us, if He was willing to give up the safety of heaven for us. Allah doesn't seem bothered to pursue such sacrifice, and Muslims will scoff at the idea of God the Son dying for us.

GOD IS UNDERSTOOD BY WHAT HE DOES

With Muslims it is helpful to point out that Jehovah often introduces himself by describing his work among His people and across the world. The book of Isaiah beams light onto Deuteronomy 6, where Jehovah reiterates who He is and what He does among the nations.

Isaiah 41:4 says, "I am the LORD, the first and with the last—I am he." This is strikingly like Jesus's statements in John 8:58 and Revelation 21:7. Isaiah 41:10 gives us more insight into God's personal engagement with us: "Do not fear, for I am with you; do not be afraid, for I am your God. I will strengthen you; I will help you; I will hold on to you with my righteous right hand." Verse 14 adds more information to Deuteronomy 6:4: "Your Redeemer is the Holy One of Israel." Verse 17 tells us of his faithfulness: "I will answer them. I am the LORD, the God of Israel. I will not abandon them."

Isaiah 42:8 says, "I am the LORD [Jehovah]. That is my name, and I will not give my glory to another or my praise to idols." This same Lord will put His Spirit onto the servant who will come to the nations—a great link to Jesus: "This is my servant; I strengthen him, this is my chosen one; I delight in him. I have put my Spirit on him; he will bring justice to the nations" (Isa. 42:1). Isaiah 61:1–3 sums it all up and is brought to fulfillment when Jesus quotes it at the beginning of His ministry (Luke 4:18–21).

In my early years debating the faith with Muslim missionaries, I would be trapped into discussing one Bible verse without the context of the rest of Scripture, but now I won't discuss Bible verses without introducing other verses to aid a deeper understanding. Memorizing these verses and telling the stories of Jesus as He lives out biblical teaching empower our conversations with Muslims.

DISCUSS AND REFLECT

1. Why is it helpful to focus on our theological differences with Islam?

2. Why is it easy to spot the differences between our religions?

3. What three areas do Muslim missionaries focus on when challenging Christianity?

4. What key Qur'anic verse points to a central doctrine about Allah, and how does it differ to Jehovah?

5. What verses can we use to show the character of the Lord to those who are not Christians?

CHAPTER 17

God's Name

"Moru, Moru! She said Allah is a he, Allah is a he!" The ten-year-old son of my Pashtun friend frantically called his mum to come and speak to us about this grave "mistake" we had just made. Our dear friends from Afghanistan knew my colleague and I were Christians, and when we spoke about the Lord with them, we were often met with kind, but clear objections to the God we loved and spoke about. For this family, Allah could not be described using any personal pronouns—Allah could not be "a he"—that is too much like a man! Allah had to remain undefined. Upon our first visit to the house, my friend had made sure that we knew, "Allah had no son." It certainly made for some interesting conversations when we spoke with members of the family about the Lord Jesus Christ.

HAS IT EVER STRUCK you how often the Lord introduces Himself by multiple names? They describe His presence and actions at a specific event in history? Those names also inform us as to *who* is speaking to us, which will be any one of the three Persons of God—the Father, the Son, or the Holy Spirit. God does not present Himself as a philosophical principle or with a theological term. He is interested in personal introductions! He gives us His name and then introduces His work, reminding us of how He has walked with His people through the ages (Judg. 2:1; 1 Sam. 10:18; Ps. 81:10).

GOD INTRODUCES HIMSELF BY NAME

Here are a few examples: He is Jehovah, who holds our hand and sets His people free from sin (Isa. 42:6–8). He forms us and we are given His name (Isa. 43:6b–7). When He introduces His personal name, He then expands on its meaning and the promises connected to it. In Exodus 3:14–18, the Lord informs Moses that He has paid close attention to the slavery the people have been under and promises He is going to do something about it. Throughout the Bible, the Lord refers to the events of this rescue and other similar actions of rescue (Num. 15:41; Deut. 5:6; Judg. 2:1; Mic. 6:4). He created us knowing He would take on our humanity and die for us! (Gen. 3:15; Luke 24:44–47). He is the only *"Savior,"* the great *"I AM,"* and there is no other god for us (Isa. 43:10–11; John 8:58). God is personal, meeting with His people throughout the Old Testament, dwelling with His people through Jesus (which means "the Lord is salvation"), and indwelling His people through the Spirit.

ALLAH IS NOT A NAME

We've talked a bit about God's character and actions, but let's go back to initial introductions. The god of Islam does not give us a name. Allah is not a name; it simply means "the god." Certainly, in the centuries since the Qur'an was written, Islam has established ninety-nine names of Allah, and they will often be seen on living room walls or in Islamic restaurants. The names are better seen as titles to which mystical spiritual power is attached, but they don't describe a personal being who interacts with human beings, though they are revered: "Allah—there is no deity except Him. To Him belong the best names" (Q 20:8; 59:24).

Not all of Allah's names are clearly found in the Qur'an; rather they are sometimes gleaned from multiple Islamic texts. While they might refer to "merciful" or "compassionate," Muslims cannot clearly explain how Allah proves this or what his actions are, as he cannot be described by human language and concepts. Muslims may refer to how Allah has given them blessings during this life, but then many non-Muslims have physical blessings today, so does Allah bless them too? This concept of general grace for all aligns closer to biblical teaching than Islamic.

The extent of the comparison between God's name and the names given to Allah is too extensive for this book,[1] but it is vital to understand that while we might recognize a few of Allah's names because they look similar to Christian titles, the meanings are vastly different.

INVOKING THE NINETY-NINE NAMES OF ALLAH

Muslims are encouraged to say the names of Allah, but when they do, they are not thinking about our Lord. "And to Allah belong the best names, so invoke Him by them. And leave [the company of] those who practice deviation concerning His names. They will be recompensed for what they have been doing" (Q 7:180).

On Islamic religious days, during the fast (called *Ramadan*), or on the pilgrimage (called *hajj*), the names of Allah are often invoked as a means of protection, blessing, and hope of reward. Many are presented with a warning not to associate anything with Allah: "He is Allah—other than whom there is no deity, the Sovereign, the Pure, the Perfection, the Bestower of Faith, the Overseer, the Exalted in Might, the Compeller, the Superior. Exalted is Allah above whatever they associate with Him" (Q 59:23).[2]

A few of the ninety-nine names of Allah use titles we would use for the Lord, though their meaning can be different, partly because the two are different in character. They are not the same being.

Consider the following names of Allah:

The Creator, the Inventor, and the Fashioner (Q 59:24). In Islam none of these titles reflect the Creator being personally involved with his creation. Does Allah create humans in his image? No, he doesn't. Does he come down to walk in his creation like God does (Gen. 3:8–15)? Never. The verse immediately jumps to how exalted he is: "Whatever is in the heavens and the earth is exalting him." Compare this with Genesis 3:8–9 where we read of the Lord's walking and speaking with Adam and Eve.

The Forgiver (Q 2:225), though not in a context of justice, as we see in the Bible. Allah's forgiveness is uncertain. Ask Muslim friends what Allah has done to make a way for his forgiveness and what he has done about evil. They will likely repeat one of Islam's mantras found at the beginning of every Qur'anic chapter except the ninth: "In the name of Allah most gracious most merciful" (*bismillāhi ir-raḥmāni ir-raḥīm*). Or refer to Qur'anic verses on forgiveness. They will focus on the ease of Allah's forgiveness.

The Knowing (Q 2:158; 4:1) is reflected in most books of the Qur'an, often connected to warnings of punishment and edicts to obey Islamic practices. It warns believers that Allah is watching them. At times the title is included in verses which allow harm to women, especially slave women: "all married women (are forbidden unto you) save those (captives) whom your right hand possess. It is a decree of Allah for you. . . . Lo! Allah is ever Knower, Wise" (Q 4:24).[3] These verses lead us to ask Muslim friends what kind of character Allah has, especially when his edict allows Muslim men to marry already married slaves. Which is why we saw such behavior with the rise of ISIS and Boko Haram.

In the Bible the knowing of God is connected to God's knowing us as His children. "But the one who boasts should boast in this: that he understands and knows me—that I am the LORD, showing faithful love, justice, and righteousness on the earth, for I delight in these things. This is the LORD's declaration" (Jer. 9:24). This verse opposes the whole concept of Allah. Allah may be "knowing," but he is to remain unknown, while God wants us to know Him!

TROUBLING NAMES OF ALLAH

Among the ninety-nine names are many that do not resonate with Christians, such as *the Proud, the Haughty* (Q 59.23).[4] A strange name to Christians as it is one of the reasons for the existence of evil in today's world. It is also the reason for our downfall. We can compare this name with the destructive sin of "pride" (Prov. 3:34; Isa. 2:12; 23:9; James 4:6;1 Pet. 5:5). "God opposes the proud but shows favor to the humble" (James 4:6 NIV). Names like these point out how different Allah is from the triune God.

Allah is called *the Grasper, the Restrainer* (Q 2:245), or *the Abaser (Degrader)* (Q 56:3). These names are not always easy to understand, and Muslim theologians will interpret them differently, though 2:245 seems to relate to Allah's withholding or granting "abundance" (wealth). As a comparison, Christians can speak of the Lord's currently restraining Satan (2 Thess. 2:7) or evidence of the Holy Spirit's dwelling in believers helping them have self-control (Gal. 5:22–23). All of which traditional Muslims will respect. An example of unrestraint leading to disobedience is found in Genesis 16 when Abraham conceives a child, Ishmael, with Hagar, a servant in the house. This is a key story for Muslims who believe Muhammad comes through the line of Ishmael. It leads on to gospel themes in Genesis 17 of the miraculous promised child through to Genesis 22, the sacrifice and then rescue of this promised child.

Allah is also *the One Who Leads Astray* (Q 4:142). The idea of fatalism, and what Allah wills, is embedded in Islamic rhetoric and vision of life: "And We did not send any messenger except [speaking] in the language of his people to state clearly for them, and Allah sends astray [thereby] whom He wills and guides whom He wills. And He is the Exalted in Might, the Wise" (Q 14:4).

Allah is also *the Hidden* (Q 57:3), which is a stark difference to the God who has worked through history to reveal who He is to us. Qur'an 57 provides a list of Allah's descriptions. Unlike the Trinity, Allah will always remain hidden, even in eternity, except for the few who will see his shin on judgment day (Q 68:42). This hidden being, who does not physically walk in our world, leads us far away from the Savior of the World.

THEOLOGY OF GOD THROUGH THE BOOK OF EXODUS

Exodus 3 and 33 provide an excellent backdrop to compare to the Islamic theology of God. In fact, the whole book of Exodus is one of the easiest books to read with Muslims.[5] Its themes challenge Islam's god as it reveals the Lord who shows up to rescue His people. It speaks of salvation. We learn about the work of the Holy Spirit. We see how the congregation is built around the activities and worship building established at the heart of the community, the place where God resides! We read of the glory of God, an invitation to a banquet with God, and the physical closeness of God to human beings. None of this is Islamic. It is as if Islam had tried to undo God's central work in history, to reconcile all human beings back to Him to live with Him as a family, as a friend (2 Cor. 5:18–21). This book is referenced throughout the Scriptures, mentioned in almost every book of the Bible. While Allah remains aloof, Exodus defines exactly who God is, from His personal name (also taken by Jesus in John 8:58) to His actions, to His love for His people and to salvation. In summary, Allah does not show up, and Jehovah does.

DISCUSS AND REFLECT

1. How does the Lord introduce Himself, especially compared to Allah?

2. Why are God's names in the Bible so important?

3. Why is there a disconnect between Allah and his names?

4. How do the titles and descriptions of Allah differ from God?

5. How does the book of Exodus and Old Testament stories help us explain who God is with Muslim friends?

CHAPTER 18

Human Beings

"Allah hears my prayers and answers me." A Muslim mission-
ary was speaking about knowing God. I asked her how Allah heard
her prayers: "Does Allah hear like we hear, or does he have eyes to
see? Does he speak as we speak?" That sounded "ridiculous" to her,
because in traditional Islam, Allah cannot be like us in any way. He
does not hear as we hear, speak as we speak, see as we see. It makes
Allah incredibly aloof and nondescript. I began to share with her
the detailed descriptions of God throughout the Bible, starting with
God's creating human beings in His image and working so that we
can physically live with Him one day. I agreed with her that human
beings are not God, but I disagreed with her when explaining we are
made in the image of God. Her Islamic theology could not accom-
modate this.

THE NATIONAL BIBLIOTECH OF Paris periodically releases beautiful tomes on ancient medieval manuscripts. Before the advent of the printing press, the pages of the Bible were illustrated by hand. Deep theology is woven through these drawings from our ancient Christian forefathers. A manuscript from fifteenth-century Paris exquisitely illustrates the Father and Son sitting together designing the world. Jesus has a compass in hand drawing the world, designing every detail of it. The Holy Spirit is ever present with them, depicted as a dove. It culminates with Jesus standing next to Adam drawing Eve out of his side.[1] While we know artists won't be able to paint a perfect depiction of the Trinity, we can see how medieval theologians delved deep into theology, much as we do today (Prov. 8:27–31; Ps. 8), to put words and images to the God of the Bible. The illustrations show a Creator personally designing us and our world. With each illustration these ancient Bibles reveal God's intricate relationship with humanity. By stark contrast, Islam, a competing theology at the time, will not depict Allah or Muhammad in art form. Muslims believe Allah created human beings, but we are *not* made in his image. Nothing in creation reflects who Allah is or how he works. Even his names, while descriptive, don't describe concrete actions. Allah does not stoop down to anything below himself, and of course becoming a human being would be just this. This is important because our theology of God informs our theology of humanity.

GOD WHO IS NEAR

Allah is considered "transcendent" in Islamic theology. He is something that is outside of us, utterly other, untouchable. Allah is hidden, subtle, unknown. Allah is not part of an eternal family. Allah has no relationship with us, no direct contact with earthlings in anything. Because Allah does not incarnate into the world, he remains aloof from humanity (Q 2:225; 6:100; 6:103; 42:11; 112:4).[2] And yet a couple verses imply that Allah is near (Q 50:16; 57:4). Muslim theologians may explain it as Allah being "near in knowledge," often added in brackets in English translations of the Qur'an, but the verses are in the context of Allah's seeing all you do, or in the context of punishment.[3] Nearness as a friend and a loving relationship is absent. In essence, Allah becomes a higher power that people seek to reach but cannot. Or if they believe they have, it is often because they have dabbled in spiritual practices to reach another spiritual dimension that we'd deem occult.

Many religions, including mystical forms of Islam, provide access to spiritual dimensions through meditations and other religious practices. Muslims often dabble in the occult (sometimes unknowingly), repeating incantations and Qur'anic chants to ignite spiritual connections, but they too do not lead to God. For this kind of Muslim, Allah may not be seen as aloof because they have had tangible spiritual experiences, but the route to these experiences is not holiness and repentance but pagan rituals. Muslims would generally agree dabbling in the occult is a dangerous practice, but since pagan rituals remain at the heart of some of the pillars, clarity on the topic becomes muddy.

The Bible confronts these types of spiritualities head-on because, while they appeal to inclinations within the human heart, they don't lead us to God (Lev. 19:31; 2 Kings 21:6; 1 John 4:1). The Bible by contrast does not put forward rituals or the occult as a pathway to God; instead it puts forward the Man from heaven (John 3:13; 1 Cor. 15:47), through whom we have access in one Spirit to God the Father (John 14:6; Eph. 2:18; Heb. 10:19).

Muslims might point out that the Bible, too, speaks of God's being transcendent. Yet even here God seeks relationship! "For as heaven is higher than earth, so my ways are higher than your ways, and my thoughts than your thoughts" (Isa. 55:9), which comes after a verse calling us to seek the Lord while He may be found, to call to Him while He is near. The whole Bible tells us God desires our faithful love, and understanding of Him more so than ritual (Hosea 6:6).

WE ARE MADE IN GOD'S IMAGE

True spirituality is found in the God who is real—the God who made us like Him. This God always has entered the world of humans (Gen. 1:2; 3:8–9). One gigantic chasm between our beliefs is found in the theology of creation and of human beings.

The creation accounts of Genesis, Job, and Psalms, with others dotted around the Scriptures, make for profound reading. There are some creation passages in the Qur'an too, but those leave out key elements of our beginnings (Q 16:4; 23:12–14; 36:77; 40:67).

Being made in God's image informs us of our value and integral connection with the God of the universe. If we are made by Allah, a being that is utterly separate from us, then we are just like other creatures—fabulous but nothing like God. If we are simply animals, we are not distinct from others. God, then, has no need to call us family, child, son, daughter, or the bride of Christ. If this is the case, there is nothing unique about a human being. Yet the Bible is all about imbuing value, meaning, and eternal life to human beings. We are made in God's image. And God makes sure to introduce this profound detail in the first chapter of the Bible!

THE TRINITY CREATED US

The Bible tells us that when God began creating the world, it wasn't just the Father working to create. All of creation is from the Father, created through the Son (Prov. 8:30–31; John 1:1–3; Col. 1:16; Heb. 1:3) in the power of the Holy Spirit, who was working to prepare and cultivate life (Gen. 1:2). Okay, we must pause here because Proverbs 8 is an amazing passage of Scripture to read with Muslims. Verses 30–31 say: "I was a skilled craftsman beside him. I was his delight every day, always rejoicing before him. I was rejoicing in his inhabited world, delighting in the children of Adam." God is creating the world, and then beside Him is another Craftsman who delights in us! We know who that must be! We know that God the Father created through His Son!

But it goes further than this. God lets us into a private discussion in Genesis 1:26: "Let us make man in our image, according to our likeness." We delight in this thought, but for those outside the Christian faith, it is tough to comprehend God's having a conversation between the Father and Son, and more so that we are made like them.

Something about humans reflects who God is in character, will, form, creativity, family, longing, and even destiny. Too often human beings try to allegorize weighty biblical statements like this, and yet when we let the Scripture speak for itself, what God is saying is clear. We are like God. God is *not* completely removed from us. As if to be sure we've got it right, the Bible summarizes the conversation God was having, by reiterating it in verse 27: "So God created man in his own image; he created him in the image of God; he created them male and female."

Psalm 139:13–14 continues to expand on God's hands-on creation of us. God knit us together in our mother's womb—each person is designed by God. Each person is "remarkably and wondrously made."

Muslim friends will counter the idea of human beings being made in God's image. They would not understand artwork that shows Jesus drawing Eve out of the side of Adam (Islamic theology does not allow for images), and the integral value of a human being is not an emphasis in the Qur'an.

A couple of Qur'anic verses are used for Muslims to support the dignity and equality of people (Q 4:1; 33:35). Qur'an 4:1 speaks of men and women coming from the womb of their mother. And Qur'an 33:35 speaks of people's good deeds being rewarded and granting them forgiveness. Qur'an 17:70 is quoted through many online Muslim discussions on the matter of dignity, though this verse is surrounded by verses on judgment, good and bad deeds: "And We have certainly honored the children of Adam and carried them on the land and sea and provided for them of the good things and preferred them over much of what We have created." In Qur'an 15:28–31, Allah speaks about creating Adam and demands the angels bow down to him, including Iblis (Satan) (Q 15:28–31). Qur'an 45:13 is also quoted in discussions about the status of human beings: "And He has subjected to you whatever is in the heavens and whatever is on the earth—all from Him." Qur'an 49:13 sums up the essence of nobility and value in the sight of God, "O mankind, indeed We have created you from male and female and made you peoples and tribes that you may know one another. Indeed, the most noble of you in the sight of Allah is the most righteous of you. Indeed, Allah is Knowing and Acquainted." So dignity and equality are connected to how we behave and whether Allah approves of us. While Muslims believe we are made by Allah, there is little detail to his feeling toward people in general.

ALLAH, THE "ROYAL WE" OF ISLAM, DOES NOT CREATE HUMANS IN HIS IMAGE

Is there any passage of the Qur'an that reflects this unique value of the human being? Not at all. What's more, human beings cannot reflect any element of God. The Qur'an states that we were fashioned from one soul and from the womb (Q 4:1). Qur'an 23:12–14 gives us some detail of the process from an Islamic perspective: "Verily We created man from a product of wet earth; Then placed him as a drop (of seed) in a safe lodging; Then fashioned We the drop a clot, then fashioned We the clot a little lump, then fashioned We the little lump bones, then clothed the bones with flesh, and then produced it as another creation. So blessed be Allah, the Best of creators!"[4]

A sidenote but often raised in conversations: when you read the Qur'an, you will often read of Allah's referring to himself as "We." It is a theological dilemma for Muslims because Allah is no "We." Allah is an "I," a singular being. He is not part of a family. When God is saying, "Let *us* make humans in our image" in the book of Genesis, it is the Trinity discussing their vision and plan for creation. Muslims might try explaining Allah's use of "we" by referring to Queen Victoria's often-attributed comment, "We are not amused," now called "the royal we." However, "the royal we" did not exist in the eighth and ninth century when the Qur'an was being written. When the Qur'an says, "We fashioned the lump," we can't read Christian theology into this; Allah does not work like the Trinity does.

The Bible is consistent in its presentation of the Trinity, and the Trinity is consistent in their interactions with people. God has always been hands on and involved, and this is seen through Jesus. Jesus came as the perfect person, to make a way for us to be like Him. Keep this man at the heart of any conversations about God when talking with Muslims.

Jesus came as the perfect person, to make a way for us to be like Him. Keep this man at the heart of any conversations about God when talking with Muslims.

DISCUSS AND REFLECT

1. Why would Muslims reject Genesis 1:26–28?

2. What is the Qur'anic teaching about the nearness of Allah?

3. How was the Trinity involved in our creation, and how is this different from Islam?

4. What Qur'anic verses are used to show "value/dignity" of human beings? How do they compare with biblical verses on the same topic?

5. How can you challenge the explanation of the "royal we" mentioned throughout the Qur'an? And why is this phrase a problem for the Islamic view of God?

CHAPTER 19

The Perfect Human Being

My delightful Kosovan Muslim neighbor asked to read the Qur'an with me. She had heard negative views of the Qur'an's teaching on women and asked me to show her the passages of the Qur'an that relate to women. We turned to each verse (Q 2:25, 222–223, 228, 230, 282; 4:1, 3, 24, 34, 128; 30:21; 33:32–33, 35, 51–59; 65:1–5). She started comparing her language with the English/ Arabic version I had and was horrified by what she read. "This is not good! I don't like this! I don't believe this is right!"

I shared with her my studies on the matter, comparing it to how Jesus spoke with women. His life was filled with wholesome friendships with men and women, many of whom went on to be key witnesses for Him when He rose from the dead and after He ascended into heaven. In His life on earth, there was no hint in His behavior and no teaching from Him that allowed abuse from men to women, no acceptance of unfaithfulness or broken relationships. His teaching and life were filled with love and respect for all those around Him, regardless of gender or age.

LET'S THINK A BIT more on this perfect man of God and contrast Him to Muhammad, Islam's perfect man. Who Jesus is and who Muhammad is provide deep insight into God's view of human beings. Since Allah is so aloof in the Qur'an and since Jesus has been removed from the heart of Islamic theology and replaced by a miracle-maker called Isa, another man has become the central being of Islam, Muhammad. He has become the epitome of what a person should be. He is the example for all to follow: "Indeed in the Messenger of Allah you have a good example to follow" (Sura 33:21; 68:4), and according to Allah, Muhammad is to be obeyed alongside him (Q 47:80).

MUHAMMAD

For many Muslims, Muhammad is the tangible link to Allah. And yet today Muhammad is not alive and no longer able to aid the Muslim follower.

Muhammad's actions reflect something of the character of Allah, as he acts as Allah's representative on earth. This is too big a topic to go in to now, but from a biblical perspective we can share with Muslims some of the reasons we do not see

Muhammad as the example for all people to follow today. Qur'an 9, which is traditionally seen as Muhammad's last sermon, is but one example of why we would not follow Muhammad and his men (also see Q 33:30–57; 66:1–5).

Muslims believe he has a role in the end times, and according to some of their traditions, he may even be able to aid Muslims in gaining access to the Islamic paradise, but he is no Savior. Though the Qur'an does not specifically say Muhammad will intercede for Muslims on judgment day, it does allude that there may be intercession, as well as saying there will be none for those destined to hell. "That Day, no intercession will benefit except [that of] one to whom the Most Merciful has given permission and has accepted his word" (Q 20:109). This kind of verse is then expanded in detail in extra-Qur'anic Islamic writings. By contrast, a verse directed to the people of Israel tells us that "no soul will suffice for another soul . . . nor will intercession be accepted from it, . . . nor will they be aided" (Q 2:48), and paradise is not attained by the "people of the book" (Christians and Jews). Help is not found in a person but only from Allah (Q 4:123). Qur'an 6:51 is clear that there is none besides Allah who will be an intercessor. "It is the Day when a soul will not possess for another soul [power to do] a thing; and the command, that Day, is [entirely] with Allah" (Q 82:19).

MUHAMMAD DID NOT SPEAK IN GOD'S NAME

Christians cannot accept Muhammad because he speaks in the name of another God, not in the name of the Holy Trinity. Deuteronomy 18:20 tells us that a prophet should not speak in the name of other gods, nor say what the LORD has not authorised. Since Muhammad speaks for Allah, the Christian can't accept Muhammad as a valid prophet or teacher. If reading this verse with Muslim friends, it can be helpful to highlight that "LORD" in our English Bibles refers to God's name *Yahweh*.

Muhammad did not come in the name of Yahweh, and he did not meet with God or walk with Him on earth. Rather, he met an angel in a cave and, through disturbing experiences, started to receive a revelation. At first, he was not sure if it was from Allah and wondered if the spirit was from Satan, but in the end he became convinced it was from Allah. According to most Islamic theologians, Allah does not have form even if the Qur'an does allude to "looking at their Lord," which presumably means he has some sort of form (Q 75:22–23), but that is not clear in Islamic theology.

GOD NOW SPEAKS THROUGH HIS SON, NOT THROUGH THE PROPHETS

There is another reason Christians don't accept Muhammad as a role model for human beings, and this we find in Hebrews 1:1–3 (author paraphrase). In this passage we are taught that "God [the Father] used to speak through the prophets at many times in and various ways. . . . Now He speaks through His Son." So there is no need for a prophet called Muhammad to come six hundred years later!

Note that Muslims won't realize that when the New Testament uses the word *God* it is usually referring to the Father. The New Testament is clear when it is speaking of Jesus referring to Him as "Christ," "Savior," "Son," "Son of Man" (Dan. 7:13; Matt. 9:6), "Son of God" (Matt. 14:33), or simply "Jesus." The Holy Spirit is usually referred to as such, or "the spirit," "Spirit of Christ," "Spirit of truth." Jesus gives the holy Spirit a wonderful description: "the Counselor/Comforter" (John 14:16). This is an important point for conversations with Muslims, as some will not realize the variety of divine titles throughout Scripture.

To sum up, Islam calls Muslims to follow a different man from Jesus. Their role model of humanity is vastly different from God's perfect human. Rather than follow the God who "took on flesh" to come to us (John 1:14; Isa. 7:14; Phil. 2:5–11) and is still alive today, Muslims are to obey Muhammad, a deceased man.

"Oh you who believe! Obey Allah, and obey the Messenger" (Sura 47:33). In essence, Muhammad has become the messiah figure of Islam.

WHY WE OBEY JESUS, NOT MUHAMMAD

We can ask probing questions about why the Qur'an asks people to obey a mere man—especially as this is a severe sin in Islam, called *shirk*. Why obey Muhammad when a person called Isa is a greater miracle worker? How can Muhammad be the perfect example of how a human being should be when there is a far more righteous example found in the Qur'anic Isa (Q 19:19) and, better still, in the biblical Jesus (2 Cor. 5:21; Heb. 4:15)?

What's more, if Muhammad is from God, why do his message and lifestyle contradict the Bible? Why did Muhammad not know God's name (Deut. 18)? Why does the Qur'an never mention Christianity's ultimate person—Jesus? Interestingly, Isa, who replaces Jesus in the Qur'an, is still alive according to Islamic theology.

Our message to Muslims is the Lord Jesus, who is at the center of the Christian's life. He is the seen face of God, the One who will be worshipped by all peoples, tribes, and nations (Dan.7:14–15; Col. 1:15; Heb. 1:1–3). He is the Creator of the heavens and earth and came to us in the flesh (Phil. 2:5–11), choosing to be one of us! Jesus is our role model, and His way leads to a life of love and joy and eternal life. Present this to a Muslim, and almost without fail you'll be in a spirited conversation about the Lord.

The Qur'an categorically denies all this. It denies the God who creates then chooses to walk and talk with us in person (Gen. 1:27–28; 3:1–15; Num. 12:8; Matt. 1:27). "Allah the Creator, the Inventor, the Fashioner" (Q 59:24) did not create humans in his image, nor does he come down to walk in his creation like God does (Gen. 3:8–15; 11:5; Exod. 19:11; 34:5–9). By contrast and repeatedly highlighted, Allah remains *unknown*, aloof.

Jesus is our role model, and His way leads to a life of love and joy and eternal life. Present this to a Muslim, and almost without fail you'll be in a spirited conversation about the Lord.

HUMANS WERE MADE FOR FRIENDSHIP WITH GOD

Christians know that God made human beings to live an eternal life with Him, to join His heavenly family. Not only does He act to make it happen, but He also sends us out to be ambassadors for heaven, to make a way for many more to live with God. "Therefore, we are ambassadors for Christ, since God is making his appeal through us. We plead on Christ's behalf, 'Be reconciled to God.' He made the one who did not know sin to be sin for us, so that in him we might become the righteousness of God" (2 Cor. 5:20–21).

Our short seventy or so years are given so that we can have a relationship with God, beginning now yet fully realized when we enter life after death. According to the Qur'an, Muslims were not made to have relationship with Allah; they are called just to serve him, to obey Allah and Muhammad (Q 3:32; 4:79–80; 9:24; 33:36); to be slaves of Allah (Q 25:63)]. For Muslims, humans exist to worship Allah: "I did not create the jinn and mankind except to worship Me" (Q 51:56). (Jinn are spirit beings, demons, or good spirits.)

Serving, worshipping, and obeying are, of course, a part of Christianity; and the recipient—God—also serves us (Isa. 53). Allah would never serve human beings. Jesus obeys His Father and honors Him, and we are called to do the same. Contrary to Islam, our service is part of living in community with God (John 14:2; Rev. 21:1–7), not as a slave to an ominous master. We become sons and daughters of God (Gal. 4:4–7), children of the heavenly Father (Rom. 8:16–17; 1 John 3:1), and we live in His house (Ps. 92:13). We are called to be coheirs (Rom. 8:17) and siblings to Jesus (Rom. 8:29). We are called to be holy and empowered by the Holy Spirit (Lev. 20:26; 1 Pet. 1:2).

The human being is deeply connected to God in Christianity. The human being is eternally separated from God in Islam.

DISCUSS AND REFLECT

1. How does Muhammad's example reflect the character of Allah?

2. The Lord Jesus Christ is the mediator for our salvation and the Holy Spirit for our prayers. How does this compare with Muhammad?

3. Why do Christians reject Muhammad as a spokesman for God?

4. What action of the Trinity rarely fails to start a conversation with Muslims?

5. A Christian's status before God is as a child of His. What is a Muslim's status before Allah? What Bible verses can you share to introduce concepts of being part of God's family?

CHAPTER 20

Sin and Suffering

An Algerian man asked me how Jesus could die on a cross for my sin. He was convinced no one can pay for our sin. When I asked if all people sinned, he agreed that they did. When I asked him if Muhammad sinned, he insistently proclaimed Muhammad didn't, nor did the other prophets. When I pointed out heinous crimes against humanity done at the direction and hands of Muhammad, he would not interpret them as sin. I pointed out that Muhammad had to ask forgiveness for sin (Q 48:1–2), which meant he had done something wrong. Yet, to the Algerian Muslim, Muhammad did not sin.

During the conversation he had highlighted how human beings were born good and children were not born with sin. Sin was learned, and we were not innately sinful. I had been praying that the Lord would break through and help him see the foundational reason for the brokenness and division so apparent throughout our societies. As he talked about the sinlessness of children and the righteousness of

on each other
in unbridled rage. One hit the other. Yells, cries, and indignation
found the boys in a tumble on the ground at our feet.

*babies, his two young boys who had been happily playing next to us
for the duration of the conversation, suddenly turned on each other
in unbridled rage. One hit the other. Yells, cries, and indignation
found the boys in a tumble on the ground at our feet.*

*I looked up at the father, pointed to the boys, spread my hands,
and said, "I believe the children are sinning." His face broke out into
a sheepish smile, and as he calmed his boys down, he spread his hands
and said, "I have nothing to say."*

THE BOYS NEED SOMEONE to intervene for them and take away their
sin. For their rage the Lord Jesus died, taking that sin upon
Himself. In Islam those boys do not have a god who makes a sure
and certain way for their sin problem to be solved.

The Lord in His mercy has given human beings just seventy
to eighty short years of life (Gen. 6:3; Ps. 90:10) to live in a world
which groans from sin's consequences. For some, those seventy
years are cut short. For others, through medical and technical
innovations, a few more years have been added, but all in all,
we have just a short, often painful start till death takes us into
eternity. God has done something about those moments of pain,
so that for those who entrust their lives to Him, it will cease, and
only happiness will prevail.

The Trinity works together to destroy all that causes pain
and suffering and even death. Our Father sent His Son Jesus to

die for us (John 3:16–17), and Jesus chose to go through with that suffering (Luke 22:42), while the Holy Spirit empowered Jesus to accomplish His work to rescue us (Heb. 9:14).

Jesus came to destroy the works of the devil. This heavenly Man is a visual living example of how far God will go to make sure evil is done away with in eternity. The same cannot be said of Muhammad, Islam's man of example.

LIFE IS A TEST IN ISLAM

Does Allah choose to suffer to save Muslims? No, Allah would not do that. What has Allah done to ensure his people have safe passage to a life with him? Nothing. Human beings are not made to live with God in Islam: "I did not create the jinn and mankind except to worship Me" (51:56).

For Muslims sin is not the reason we are still living in a broken world. Life in Islamic theology is a test (Q 76:3), so that Allah may try them. "And We will surely test you with something of fear and hunger and a loss of wealth and lives and fruits, but give good tidings to the patient" (Q 2:155). If Muslims successfully pass life's test, which is one reason for sin and suffering, they might gain the possibility of living in a garden after death, a place where immorality will continue, this time as a gift from Allah (Q 37:44–48).

This current suffering life seems to be a consequence of Allah's forgiveness. The Qur'an tells us of the fall of the first man and woman, Adam and his wife. In Islam she is usually called Huwa. Allah calls all people to bow down to Adam, but Satan, sometimes called Iblis in Islam, refuses to bow down to him (Q 7:11). Allah casts him down, and Satan threatens to wait for humans on Allah's "straight path." Adam and his wife are put in paradise (Q 7:16). Once tempted by Satan, they make a misstep and realize they have no clothes on (Q 7:20–22). They beg Allah's forgiveness. He forgives them, and they are then cast down to earth. They are clothed and told how to live. That initial sin of our foreparents is not connected to a broken relationship in Islam. Stories of Allah walking with his people are not a part of Qur'anic theology. Sin did not break a relationship with Allah. Apart from when Allah spoke to Adam before the fall, he doesn't walk with human beings, and he doesn't plan to. They are not in friendship.

PROPHETS WITH THEIR BOOKS GUIDE EACH GENERATION

So, how does Allah help Muslims keep away from the things Islam considers sin? Muslims believe each generation of people receives a prophet, and their prophets have specific books—for the Jews the Torah, for the Christians the Injil (a version of the Gospels, though Muslims tell us it no longer exists), for

Muslims the Qur'an. The Qur'an is supposed to confirm the previous books, though Muhammad is called to judge between them with the Qur'an being the standard (Q 5:48). The previous books, such as the Torah and Injil, were given as a guiding light for their time (Q 5:44–47), but now the Qur'an is seen as the final revelation. Where there are disagreements between the texts, the Qur'an is to be followed. Each prophet and book are sent to guide their people back to Allah, to deny any son of god (Q 4:171), or any associates (Q 5:72), to proclaim Islamic views of Allah and the last day, and to adhere to Islamic rituals (Q 9:18). Prayer, fasting, giving, and jihad are highlighted throughout the Qur'an (Q 2:43; 2:177) and are one way a person might be forgiven.

SIN IN ISLAM

The Qur'an highlights different sins and detailed rules to annul them. They are then expanded upon in the teaching and example of Muhammad and in Islamic law. Overcoming sin is done by adhering to Islamic practices and beliefs, going through the motions of Islam with good intentions.

There are major and minor sins. Associating others with God is repeatedly emphasized and seen by Muslims as a severe sin. Christians would agree with Muslims that associating something with God, as in calling a created thing divine, is a grievous sin that belittles God. In Islam this sin is called *shirk*, and Muslims believe Christians have committed shirk alongside those who have multiple gods. To them Jesus has been elevated from being a created human to a deity, not realizing that the Scriptures teach Jesus is the Lord who came down to us, and He is our Creator. Since Islam has no room for a God who comes down to us, it is understandable that Jesus is a stumbling block for them.

Fornication, alcohol, usury (interest in banks) are often mentioned as major sins by Muslims when asked what sin is.

The word *sin* is often understood by Muslims as sexual indiscretions, so we may need to clarify that in Christian theology sin is an overall word for any wrongdoing. Muslims will often speak of sin versus mistakes, or of major and lesser sins, though the terms *wrongdoing/wrongdoer* often connected with disbelievers is a key focus in the Qur'an (Q 2:150).

PRECARIOUS FORGIVENESS, ETERNAL SIN

In Islam, committing a sin doesn't eternally separate a person from Allah. The Qur'an seems to imply that Allah forgives easily, and many Muslim friends attest to this. "Say: Oh, My servants who have transgressed against themselves [by sinning], do not despair of the mercy of Allah. Indeed, Allah forgives all sins. Indeed, it is He who is the Forgiving, the Merciful" (Q 39:53).

The last clause of this verse is repeated throughout the Qur'an, and yet Muslims cannot be sure Allah will forgive them on the last day, especially if they commit a major sin.

Qur'an 25:68–70 explains sins Allah will not forgive but ends with: "Except for those who repent, believe and do righteous work. For them Allah will replace their evil deeds with good." The big question Muslims are left with is whether their righteous work will have been enough to replace their bad.

Muslim friends speak of practicing good deeds, like faithful prayers, serious fasting, fasting more than required, giving to charity to cover minor sins, and seeking forgiveness from Allah. Committing minor sins may not expel you from paradise: "If you avoid the major sins which you are forbidden, We will remove from you your lesser sins and admit you to a noble entrance [into Paradise]" (Q 4:31). What's more, following Muhammad shows love for Allah who in return "will love you and forgive you your sins. And Allah is Forgiving and Merciful" (Q 3:31). The ease of Allah's forgiveness toward humans shows he has little justice, and yet Allah is quick to meter out judgment on those who do not follow Islam or follow it correctly. We can see this in how he dealt with Adam and Huwa. When they sinned, they were forgiven, yet they were still thrown out of the garden to be tested. No promise of a final dealing with sin is given, as was given to Adam and Eve in the Bible (Gen. 3:15).

Forgiveness is only hoped for, and reward is awarded to those who practice Islam correctly. Qur'an 4:136 emphatically states that if they do not believe in Allah, his angels and his messengers and the last day, then they have strayed into error. Muslims will say to Christian friends that they can be forgiven and rewarded if they believe in Allah and Islam's last day (Q 5:69). The Qur'an often refers to Islamic angels, Islamic messengers, and the Islamic last day—all of which deny the Trinity, the divinity of Jesus and His death on the cross, and life with God in eternity.

Perhaps the biggest question a Christian has about sin in Islam is why there is sin in paradise and eternal separation from Allah? It begs the question whether we would want Allah's forgiveness if our ultimate destiny were a life filled with sexual sin given as an eternal reward.

DISCUSS AND REFLECT

1. In Islam, is sin the reason we live in a broken world?

2. What Qur'anic verses speak about the fall of human beings? How would you biblically respond to them?

3. What is Islam's view of the prophets and their role in tackling sin?

4. How is the Islamic view of sin understood in comparison to biblical teaching?

5. Does the Qur'an offer a final solution to sin?

CHAPTER 21

Salvation

A fiery-haired Irish Muslim missionary was enjoying an aggressive interaction with a Nigerian brother who was asking him why he converted to Islam. In parrot-like fashion the Muslim missionary spat out his issues with the Trinity, including rhetoric of the trans-Atlantic slave trade, forgetting the ongoing thirteen-hundred-year-Pan-African-Islamic slave trade. His focus was on the rewards he hopes to receive in paradise. He didn't care that his religion taught sexual slavery both here and in the hereafter (Q 4:3b; 33:52). He was thrilled he would receive more wives and other women after his death. The debauched Islamic descriptions of the afterlife fueled every lustful thought of his obviously God-forsaken heart. Salvation from sin was not his to have.

The Nigerian Christian stood appalled at the audacious descriptions of sin awaiting Muslims. His own future was assured and sin free, and available to all who believed in the Christ he loved.

JESUS IS FAITHFUL, AND He is faithful to forgive us our sins (1 John 1:9) because He has intervened on our behalf and dealt with our sin: "But if anyone does sin, we have an advocate with the Father—Jesus Christ the righteous one. He himself is the atoning sacrifice for our sins, and not only for ours, but also for those of the whole world" (1 John 2:1–2). This is a profound verse to share with Muslims. What's more, Jesus Christ sustains us, as those who are hidden in Him, while the Spirit seals us for eternity. We are held in salvation by God Himself. He has interceded and He continues to intercede. Terms such as "hidden with Christ" (Col. 3:3) and "sealed with the . . . Holy Spirit" (Eph. 1:13) may need some explanation, as we don't want Muslim friends to impose Islamic theology onto these wonderful ideas. Allah is "hidden," and Muhammad is the "seal of the prophets," and yet the Bible speaks of "sealing" long before the Qur'an came along. The biblical meanings point to an ongoing action of God which promises the Christian an assurance of belonging to the Lord, something Islam does not offer Muslims.

DOES ALLAH RESCUE MUSLIMS FROM SLAVERY AND SIN?

In the English translation of the Qur'an, Allah is called perfect and holy (Q 59:23), yet how is Allah perfect and holy? From a biblical perspective, his edicts would not support this claim. Consider the following examples: polygamy (Q 4:3); domestic violence (Q 4:34); murder of unbelievers (Q 5:32); obedience to a man alongside Allah (shirk?) (Q 33:36); Muhammad's marriage to his adopted son's wife (Q 33:37); decapitation and slavery of unbelievers (Q 47:4); sexual slavery and favoritism toward Muhammad (Q 33:50).

If Allah exempted Muhammad from a standard of morality, including breaking his promises, is he able to faithfully forgive sins (33:37; 66:1–5)? There are no clear answers for Muslims to these questions, and while forgiveness is connected to a pseudo life after death, it does not lead to true transformative holiness and salvation from sinful behavior.

Can Allah save people from sin and to a life with him? On a purely practical note, would Allah be able to work in history to rescue people? He has no son (Q 18:4–5), and therefore if Allah died on the cross, the Father and Holy Spirit would not exist to aid the son and to keep the universe going. The Holy Trinity is a family who engages the world through different roles yet as one. Since Allah is a singular being who lives in eternal transcendence and nothing in creation can connect to him, it would be "beneath him" to act physically in history.

Does Islam offer freedom and assurance of salvation? Not at all. People are considered slaves when they become Muslims, bound by law, working toward gaining reward. Salvation is not a Qur'anic concept; rather the focus is on repeated warnings about hell and rewards in both this life and the one to come. Muslims must earn their place in paradise.

How does Allah plan to deal with evil in the world once and for all? Muslims believe Islam is the solution to wrongdoing, and the Qur'an is "guidance," "warner," "revelation" "wise and praiseworthy" (Q 41:1–46). It points to Muhammad (inferred by its reference to previous messengers) as the "possessor of forgiveness and . . . painful penalty" (Q 41:43), and yet this same man was allowed to break Islamic standards, and more so biblical. Though this makes sense if Allah also allows sin into paradise (Q 55:56–58), though not called sin by Islam. Allah does not act to solve the problem of sin. "Every soul earns not [blame] except against itself, and no bearer of burdens will bear the burden of another. Then to your Lord is your return" (Q 6:164). Muslims believe no person can take our sin on himself. In Islam, Christ cannot die on the cross so we can be free from sin to receive the ultimate gift—life lived with God.

The Qur'an implies that all people will taste hell; then some will be taken out of it (Q 3:185; 19:71–72). Hell is mentioned in 107 out of 114 surahs in the Qur'an. The Bible also mentions hell, but its focus is redemption when true[1] Christians are rescued from sin and evil to live an eternity without it. God gave us book after book—now in one volume, the Bible—to help us understand how sin is at the heart of the suffering of the world. God knows creation is groaning to be released from this sin, and He knows how it separates us from Him and from one another. The climax of the Bible is God's sacrifice to solve this terrible blight at the heart of our suffering.

The Qur'an frequently warns about "the last day." It is a core belief that all Muslims must accept. But in Islam that last day is judgment day with maybe a glimpse of Allah and then, for some, direct access into the garden, though for many, it will be via hell.

The Bible also has a judgment day, and Revelation 19 is well worth a read with Muslim friends on the matter. The Bible also proclaims the glorious news of a better day coming, a life that will be good and delightfully lived (Rev. 21:1–6). We will be rescued from the current broken world to an incredible life—*without* sin!

SIN CONTINUES INTO THE ISLAMIC PARADISE

In Islam there is no rescue from sin because sin continues into paradise. It is not described as such in the Qur'an, but the biblically minded person can't help but be struck by the depravity of the lifestyle of paradise and the rewards Allah outlines in the Qur'an (Q 38:49–53) and throughout Islamic literature. This does not paint a picture of a god I wish to follow or trust with forgiveness.

The final decision of what happens with Muslims lies with Allah. And for him to forgive is to allow you into a "paradise" where sin continues. That's no paradise to me. Sin has caused the world enough pain.

An uncertainty settles in Muslim minds as to their ultimate destiny when the Qur'an describes certain aspects of Allah. The root word in Arabic (makara) means deception. It is also translated as plotters, or schemers (Q 3:54; 8:30). Allah is also described as the greatest of all *plotters*, or *schemers* (Qur'an 3:54; 8:30; 10:21; 13:33). Modern-day English translations turn the word *schemer* into "planner" or say Allah is "above scheming," but this is an incorrect translation. "Allah leads astray" people as he chooses (Q 4:88; 6:39; 13:27, 33; 14:4; 16:37, 93; 17:97). Islam teaches a fatalistic view of life so that if Allah wills something, it will be done no matter what you try to do (Q 2:20, 70, 85, 253). This makes life uncertain for Muslims because Allah is unknowable and his view of sin is not consistent: what is right for one person may not be for another. Muhammad is an example of this (Q 33:50). What is sin on earth is no longer sin in heaven—as per our discussion on the female companions of paradise. Islam does not provide a consistent view of sin, which creates confusion for the follower, which doesn't really matter since human beings have no choice in any matter according to the Qur'an (Q 2:7, 20, 70; 22:16; 24:21, 46; 28:56; 33:37; 35:8; 39:36; 42:13). This would make sense if Muslims were slaves of Allah rather than children. Slaves have no choice in life. Children, brothers, brides, and family do make choices, all of which describes Christians in their relationship with God.

DISCUSS AND REFLECT

1. Will Muslims be saved from sin in the Islamic paradise?

2. Does Muhammad's example aid Muslims to live holy lives?

3. Does Islam offer assurance of salvation?

4. In Islam can a person stand in the place of another to redeem them from sin? What Qur'anic verses support your answer?

5. Is Allah reliable in how he deals with sin and people's eternity?

CHAPTER 22

Eternity

A petite university student clothed in long flowing robes and crowned with a tight black hijab around her face shared with me her conversion story to Islam. She had become a Muslim three years earlier. I asked her what had convinced her to become a Muslim. Her reasons focused on the monotheism of Allah and the religious practices she was following. I then asked her what the end goal was for Muslims once this life is over? What was waiting for her in eternity? She hesitated in her response, then simply stated, "I haven't studied that part of my religion yet." Her answer has stayed with me for years as I wonder why someone would convert to a religion when they don't know what their destiny will be. I wonder if she knows she will never live with God if she remains a Muslim. Sadly, she did not want to engage in a conversation on the matter.

WHY FOLLOW A RELIGION if you are not sure what life after death is like? She, like many in the world today, does not consider the consequences of our actions here and now. To outsiders Islam looks like a here-and-now religion, with much of its teaching focused on Islamic practices. It may speak of rewards in paradise, but it is not a Muslim's primary focus.

I once asked a Muslim missionary what would be waiting for me in paradise if I became a Muslim. He answered, "Whatever you wish for!" Somewhat concerned, I asked what a person would receive if their wishes were sinful. "In paradise it is not sinful. Allah will fulfill your desires" (Q 36:55–58; 41:31–32; 50:35). He was right: the Qur'an affirms his statement on multiple occasions.

DISTURBING REWARDS IN THE ISLAMIC PARADISE

When specific rewards are given in the Qur'an, the rewards are male orientated or, more accurately expressed, descriptive of a man wishing to sin sexually. Islamic paradise is described in lurid detail in Islamic literature. It makes for uncomfortable reading. The minds which devised the Islamic paradise must have moved in squalid muck. No holy person can accept that paradise.

Sadly, such places already exist across our globe, in red-light districts or high-end brothels, from Turkish harems to Las Vegas and London's prostitute rings. The detailed portrayals in Islamic traditions, like those from Muhammad's conversations with his men, through to end times theological treatises by Muslims today, don't belong in our minds, so we will stick with a few Qur'anic verses which are not so obscene, though still disturbing.

Qur'an 44:51–55 says, "Indeed, the righteous will be in a secure place; Within gardens and springs, Wearing [garments of] fine silk and brocade, facing each other. Thus. And We will marry them to fair women with large, [beautiful] eyes. They will call therein for every [kind of] fruit—safe and secure." The Qur'an describes a garden filled with couches with precious stones, paradise's inhabitants leaning back and being served by immortal youths, enjoying drink which does not cause headaches or dull their senses, fruit and meat from birds of their choice. "And [for them are] fair women with large, [beautiful] eyes, the likeness of pearls well-protected, As a reward for what they use to do" (Q 56:10–23).

In the biographies of Muhammad, he would discuss Allah's gifts this side of eternity with his men, and they are not far from what awaits them after death.[1] Women and girls are always part of the package, as are young men who wait on them. We see this throughout history in the treatment of European and African slaves in Spain and North Africa,[2] in Turkey's horrific abuse harems, and in modern-day stories that now and then slip out of the Arab and Asian world. It has always been evident in Islamic lands because it is a part of Islam's merit system, affirmed and at times gifted directly from Allah (Q 4:3; 4:24; 33:37–52; 66:1–5).

Christians who truly follow Christ work to nurture societies filled with protection for the most defenseless. Christians who are eternity focused take on board God's care for the vulnerable and those abandoned, orphaned, or widowed (Exod. 22:22–23; Ps. 68:5; James 1:27). Christianity endeavors is to set people free from all kinds of slavery (slavery to sin, self, and others; Isa. 61:1–3; Philem.), not enslave them further. The freedom found in Christ here is fully realized once we live with Him in eternity. Yet it starts now, contrary to Islam.

Christians who truly follow Christ work to nurture societies filled with protection for the most defenseless.

Muslims do have a way to look after orphans (Q 4:3) and widows in their community. Muhammad exemplified this by marrying or giving them to his men, although he was often also the reason for the need since during his lifetime women were widowed and orphaned at his command and through the actions of his men. And while there will be no need to fight in the afterlife, the behavior with women is carried into the Islamic afterlife.

When Christians go to God after death, we are safe (John 6:27; Eph. 1:13–14). Muslims don't have safety, and according to Islamic tradition they must cross a razor-sharp bridge from where they might fall into hell.[3] Whereas the Christian enters His presence and finally rests from life's troubles upon earthly death. We wait to join Him on that triumphant day, to be united with those who have gone ahead of us (1 Thess. 4:17). When a Muslim journeys after death, some believers go to the garden, while others who have sinned will fall into hell to be tortured to work off their sins (Q 3:185; 19:71–72). The disbelievers will remain there (Q 2:104; 5:37; 18:53), unable to earn their way out through their work. Some jinn and human beings were created for hell (Q 7:178–179) and would never be able to access Islam's eternal garden.

"Humans were made for eternity" was oft repeated in our small London church. We were made to live forever, not just in spirit, but our very being, our person, our mind, spirit, and body. Ecclesiastes 3:11 tells us that God has "put eternity in [our] hearts." Currently, each body has a brokenness, which will one day never face death or pain again. Yet we are eternal, and our full being will enter Christ's home. Even Christ's resurrected body bears the scars of His death (Luke 24:39–40). They point to a wonderful point in history that reminds us of His past pain for our future healed life.

A Muslim's body will be gathered according to the Qur'an: "From the earth We created you, and into it We will return you, and from it We will extract you another time" (Q 20:55). The day of resurrection in Islam is not like the day of resurrection for Christians, nor does the Qur'an contain the immense detail found in the Bible: "Allah causes you to live, then causes you to die; then He will assemble you for the Day of Resurrection, about which there is no doubt, but most of the people do not know" (Q 45:26).

Muslims are not resurrected to the eternity Christ promised. People who are given the record of their life in the right hand will enter the Islamic garden. Those who receive the record in their left hand will enter hell (Q 69:13–33). Muslims pray for forty days after their loved one has departed, begging Allah to grant mercy to their soul and access to the garden.

RELATIONSHIP AND LIFE WITH GOD

Both the Old and New Testaments speak about that wonderful day when believers rise out of the grave: "Your dead shall live; their bodies shall rise. You who dwell in the dust, awake and sing for joy! For your dew is a dew of light, and the earth will give birth to the dead" (Isa. 26:19 ESV). First Corinthians 15:51–54 describes the wonderful moment our bodies will be transformed to become imperishable and immortal. John 14:1–3 is a cherished promise from the Lord of His work for us once He goes back to heaven after His death and resurrection. He goes ahead, as if He is paving the way for us, and is building homes for us now: "If I go away and prepare a place for you, I will come again and take you to myself, so that where I am you may be also" (John 14:3). It is no wonder that Jesus starts this promise by telling his disciple and us to not be troubled (John 14:1). It is spoken as a husband who has given his all to provide a family home to live a wonderful life in, and that's exactly what it is! Our bridegroom is building our eternal home.

Muslims often shudder at the thought of God's being described as a spouse to the church, yet it is powerful imagery and helpful to reference when sharing the intimacy and depth of the Son of God's relationship with us (Eph. 5:31–32; Rev. 19:7–10). Both the Old and New Testaments use marriage as an illustration to describe the faithfulness or unfaithfulness of God's people (Hosea 2:16; 2 Cor. 11:2). Biblical marriage is different from Islamic marriage. In Islam it is more transactional, hence the struggle for Muslims to understand how our relationship with God can be described in marital terms (Isa. 54:5). The main reward Allah offers in the afterlife is women for men. Whereas God offers a far greater life, where marriage will not be thought of because life and relationships with God will be far superior.

While Allah offers rewards for his people and welcomes souls into his garden (Q 89:27–30), God Himself comes to live with His people and promises a garden city where He will dwell, with healing rivers and gardens, yes, but not where debauchery dwells (Rev. 21:8). In contrast to the Islamic paradise, it will be filled with people who have no temptations and no struggle with sin, free from our weakest self, and free to live in goodness and holiness. It will be a place of light, where no dark alleyways of evil exist. We will no longer have pain, mourning, or death. The order of events and some specifics will differ depending on different theologies, but descriptions remain the same for all Christians—peace will exist among all creatures—lambs will be safe in the presence of wild animals, as will children (Isa. 11:6–9). All that is sinful and evil will pass, and life will begin afresh (Rev. 21:1–7). That means friendship with God (John 15:15; James 2:23), friendship with one another, celebrations with food and wine (Isa. 25:6; Matt. 26:29; Luke 12:37; Rev. 19:9), and our Creator serving us (Luke 12:37; Matt. 20:28). At some point we will reign with Christ (Rev. 20:4–6). What a future!

This is a future we want every Muslim friend to join us in. The rewards from God to His people are not overflowing with the Qur'an's debauched visions of wine, women, and boys in gardens. No, God has planned for humanity a far grander eternal life. Allah plans to turn current human sin into normative life-styles in eternity, in contrast to God's vision to destroy sin once and for all so we are free to live the life we were created to live.

Our bodies will rise, and Christians will return to God. Our whole person is important and valuable to God. Our bodies will be eternal. What a day that will be, when those of us who hurt with wounds and broken limbs will be healed and whole—walking, dancing, speaking, singing, living a life only now dreamed of. God's work at this moment in time is intimate and physical. Islamic theology cannot cope with this aspect of the biblical God. It is one of the reasons Muslims reject God's Son.

For the handful of verses which mention a "return to him," no modern-day Muslim theologian presents a clear picture of a *physical* dwelling place *with* God. There may be reference to a presence (Q 54:55), or a "beholding" of Allah, but never a dwelling with Allah. Allah is not remotely interested in living in person with Muslims throughout eternity. This test he puts them through, called life, does not end with life lived in a garden city called "peace" (the meaning of Jerusalem—Rev. 21:2) built by His hands, where He will come down to physically dwell with humanity.

Muslims may point out a few Qur'anic verses which say Muslims will go to Allah: "Every soul will taste death. And We test you with evil and with good as trial; and to Us you will be returned" (Q 21:35; 28:70), but this return is unclear at best.

Islamic theology does not have a theology of God living with Adam and his wife at the beginning of human life, and so it is not clear what Muslims will be "returning to." Muslims who pursue a mystical vision of religion, like Sufis, may have a higher view of returning to Allah (or divine plural beings if "us" is literal in the Qur'an), but the Qur'an never describes a paradise where Allah lives together with humans. Muslims will only look on Allah on the last day, and the pious will be in a seat of honor, near to the "Sovereign" (Q 54:55). Yet, if Allah is not a physical being and there's no theology of him living with his people, this setup seems to speak of an impossible riddle. To understand ambiguous Islamic theology, or conflicting Qur'anic descriptions, Muslims turn to Islamic theologians who write reams of literature called "Tafsir." These are interpretations and commentaries on the Qur'an, traditionally held in a much higher status to Christian commentaries. "Returning" to Allah (Q 2:156; 5:48) is usually interpreted as resurrection and compensation after death (Q 3:185) or drawing near spirituality (Q 39:54).

The worst part of the Islamic paradise is the absence of God's making a home with human beings. Muslims, according to their own theology, will never live with Allah. The debauchery awaiting Muslims in their paradise has led me on a bolder day to say to Muslim friends that I understand why God would not reside in such a place. God does not tolerate sin, and He certainly would not give it to us as a gift.

It is a grave situation to be in, to reject the Holy Trinity, as all Muslims have. It means Muslims are eternally separated from God unless they turn from their sin and embrace the Savior. It leaves us grieving for our Muslim friends for whom God died!

DISCUSS AND REFLECT

1. Why is the Qur'anic claim that "Allah will fulfill your desires" troublesome?

2. What is troubling about the rewards Muslims will receive in paradise?

3. Why is it a place God cannot reside?

4. Will Muslims be able to escape hell?

5. What Bible verses and details would you use to explain relationship with God for eternity?

The King of Kings

"*Then I saw heaven opened, and there was a white horse. Its rider is called Faithful and True, and with justice he judges and makes war. His eyes were like a fiery flame, and many crowns were on his head. He had a name written that no one knows except himself. He wore a robe dipped in blood, and his name is called the Word of God. The armies that were in heaven followed him on white horses, wearing pure white linen. A sharp sword came from his mouth, so that he might strike the nations with it. He will rule them with an iron rod. He will also trample the winepress of the fierce anger of God, the Almighty. And he has a name written on his robe and on his thigh: KING OF KINGS AND LORD OF LORDS.*"* (Rev. 19:11–16, emphasis added)

THE RIDER ON THE white horse will finally cut through the noise of conflicting opinions and angry rhetoric, which currently numbs our senses. As we witness the extremes of modern attitudes, the world seems more divided than ever before, and our media and news bulletins add fuel to the brewing fires around the globe.

Tensions run high throughout communities worldwide. The situation looks dire.

Fourteen hundred years ago, Islam[1] entered the world stage. Whole communities were wiped out or removed, and Islam set up home. Parts of those lands have never been returned to their people, largely in Africa, Arabia, and Asia.[2] Many now call themselves "Muslim," but that is not their heritage. So, how is this different from the man of war who will come at the end times and finally bring peace?

Power movements of people rise and fall. They last for a moment failing to bring justice then lasting peace. They can never root out the key problems—and human depravity. While these still exist, none of our political world leaders will fully succeed, even though they may provide a positive environment for a while. Yet there *is* a Leader who will bring all the solutions we seek.

COUNTERFEIT LEADERS

A traditional Muslim reading this will say they will bring in the Caliphate, as Islam is the religion of peace. They are holding out for a final war, with a returning messiah-type figure who will bring the world under Islam. It has biblical overtones, but it is speaking of a religion and people of war that do not come from our heavenly Father. Biblically speaking it is a counterfeit. Counterfeit beliefs are attractive to many, as they take a good original idea and spin it with new content that has nothing to do with its originator. This counterfeit is dangerous, providing no eternal solution. It is why the Lord tells us to be careful of false prophets (Matt. 7:15–20). Remember Jesus's great Sermon on the Mount warning us, for "you'll recognize them by their fruit" (Matt. 7:16).

THE SOLUTION

Yet the Lord has a plan for humans to live forever. He will conduct one final war against sin, and He will not tolerate sin on any level. He has seen the harm it has caused society, the divide it puts between us, and He will do something about it. Jesus died for His enemies, while Muhammad killed his enemies. The Lord calls us into a friendship with Him and invites us to live with Him, yet Allah is no friend and is not currently building an extension on his home for us. Jesus fights at the end to make sure counterfeit religions can no longer lead His creation to a place where He does not dwell. He asks one thing of us: "Trust Me." That's it. And when we do, we have full certainty that He will say to us, "Well done good and faithful servant. Enter My gates. Come eat at My banquet, and let Me serve you." I'm paraphrasing, but it's all there in the Scriptures (Matt. 25:23; Luke 12:37; 22:28–29; Rev. 19:7–9).

Allah would never serve and is not interested in banqueting with us. He likely can't eat, as to Muslims that is what created things do, not Allah. Islam's vision of eternity is directly judged on the last pages of the Bible: "Salvation, glory, and power belong to our God, because his judgments are true and righteous, because he has judged the notorious prostitute who corrupted the earth with her sexual immorality; and he has avenged the blood of his servants that was on her hands" (Rev. 19:1–2). Islam's immoral eternity and revenge on its enemies will not be tolerated by the King of kings. It sounds tough, but the judgment comes from the only person who can see all things and has access to the knowledge of all things. It is also given by the only person to die for all humanity.

THAT WE MAY BE SAVED TOGETHER

This book is written to help Christians understand Islam to better equip us to speak about the King of kings and Lord of lords with every Muslim we meet. What a good day it is when Muslim friends can know they are saved as they turn away from Islam and enter the eternal family of Christ. So with the Old Testament saints (Heb. 11–12:3) we together can proclaim we are "not ashamed of the gospel, because it is the power of God for salvation to everyone who believes, first to the Jew, and also to the Greek" (Rom. 1:16–17).

Revelation 21:1–7 is a beautiful promise to read with Muslims. We read of the city of peace (Jerusalem) coming down from heaven in a new heaven and earth. The great division between the heavens and earth will be removed. God will speak from the throne, proclaiming to us that He will now live with us! Death, grief, and pain will disappear. God will personally take our tears and replace our sorrow with joy (Isa. 61:1–3).

The "one seated on the throne" sums up for us what the Bible is all about: "They will be his peoples, and God himself will be with them and will be their God" (Rev. 21:3–4). In this place the Lord God Almighty, the Father, and His Son, the Lamb, are on the thrones, and their kingdom is illuminated with their light. The nations will walk by their light. The kings of the earth will bring their glory to it, and no competing lesser kings will try to rob God of His glory. And its gates will always be flung wide open, as the darkness of night will not exist. The glory and honor of the nations join it and do not oppose Him, and nothing false or detestable enters those gates. It is a protected place for God's family made up of the nations (Rev. 21:22–27).

It is a place we long to share with all our Muslim friends, and even those not counted as friends—those who follow the path of jihadis—to confess with us our sins because "he is faithful and righteous to forgive us our sins and to cleanse us from all unrighteousness" (1 John 1:9).

We address mistruths in Western society and introduce Muslims to the King of kings on the throne. We explain our differences so that they can hear the goodness of the gospel. We explain the path connecting to Abraham for eternal purposes. We start with biblical truth as we engage with religious ideas found outside the Bible. Journeying through Old and New Testament teaching, we speak of the Lord we know personally. We put Christ at the center of our discussions with Muslims and delight in the Holy Trinity in exciting conversations with those who don't yet trust the Lord. We do this in response to the declaration of the Lord Jesus, "Yes, I am coming soon" (Rev. 22:20). And so together our message cries out: "'Come!' Let anyone who hears, say, 'Come!' Let the one who is thirsty come. Let the one who desires take the water of life freely" (Rev. 22:17).

DISCUSS AND REFLECT

1. How is Islam's history—their man of war Muhammad—different from the man of war promised in Revelation 19:11–16?

2. Why are counterfeit religions attractive and dangerous?

3. How would you tell Muslims that Jesus is the solution to sin and it's a consequence of a broken society?

4. How are Allah and God different when it comes to banquets?

5. How has and how will the King of kings make all things right?

Notes

Chapter 2

1. We refer to this example because it will be raised by Muslims in conversation with Christians.

2. Quotes from the Qur'an are taken from Sahih International, accessed April 6, 2023, https://corpus.quran.com.

Chapter 3

1. Aaron W. Hughes, *Abrahamic Religions: On the Uses and Abuses of History* (Oxford, Eng.: Oxford University Press, 2012), 57.

2. Mark Durie, *The Abrahamic Fallacy*, 1 February 2014, (https://markdurie.com/the-abrahamic-fallacy/). More on the topic in his book: Mark Durie, *Which God? Jesus, the Holy Spirit, God in Christianity and Islam* (Deror Books 2nd ed., 2014), and, Mark Durie, *The Third Choice: Islam, Dhimitude and Freedom* (Deror Books, 1st ed., 2010).

3. This is an Islamic claim, not necessarily an historical claim.

4. There may be some tribes in Arabia whose blood line goes back to Abraham, and Muslims certainly claim that Muhammad's does, but this is a claim without historical support.

Chapter 4

1. Edicts can change if the Islamic law does not address a modern situation, and this is when Islamic jurists will inform Muslims of a new interpretation or application of Islamic law. This is often called a *fatwa,* which is a formal ruling by a recognized Islamic authority on points of Islamic law. Note, Muslims will have different opinions about who is authoritative. More on this in part 3.

Chapter 5

1. *Parakleto,* which can mean "counselor," "comforter," "helper," or "advocate," is found in John 14:15, 25; 15:26. Muslims change this to *periklutos,* which they say means "praised one," the same as *ahmad* in Arabic and used of Muhammad. No Bible text uses this second spelling and to add it to the Bible is a mishandling of the text.

2. Infamous Islamic preachers travel through the Islamic world teaching Muslims how to challenge the Bible and core Christian teaching. Few Christians do likewise toward Islam, which is why we need more biblically sound resources to meet the challenges posed against our faith.

Chapter 6

1. Though the Qur'an uses some biblical elements, like the creation of Adam (Qur'an 2:30–38; 7:11–27) and Moses at the burning bush and with Pharoah (Qur'an 20:9–99; 27:7–14; 28:29–43), they leave out the most important details. Apart from the story of Moses, most Qur'anic verses contain only fragments of the original stories, Islamize them (such as replacing Jehovah with Allah, Qur'an 20:98; 27:15), and mix them up with other Bible stories, sometimes from completely different time periods of history. Haman, from the time

of Esther (fifth century BC), turns up alongside Pharoah (thirteenth to fourteenth century BC) in the Qur'an (Qur'an 28:38; 40:36–37).

2. For more on this topic and an evangelism aid, see my book written with Tim Dieppe: *Questions to Ask Your Muslim Friends: A Closer Look at Islamic Beliefs and Texts* (London: Wilberforce Publications, 2022).

3. The God of the Bible, the true God, doesn't *just* visit His people; He came to dwell with His people through Christ and indwells His people through the Spirit. This concept of a God who visits His people is an excellent conversation point as you talk with friends who are Muslims because Allah would never visit his people.

4. Though Qur'anic verses also encourage patience or forgiveness, leaving Muslims the option to enact revenge or to forgive.

5. Note that the Qur'an does not provide all the details of how Muslims fast. This is found in Islamic law and the life of Muhammad, which are now at the heart of Islamic practice.

6. See the lists of Muhammad's battles and murders done by his men compiled by Bernie Power in his book, *Understanding Jesus and Muhammad* (Alma, MI: Morning Star Publishing, 2015), 90–96.

7. The bracketed clauses seen in Qur'ans are additions from Islamic interpreters, gleaned from Islamic commentaries through the centuries.

Chapter 7

1. Muslims must recite in Arabic every day: "There is no deity but Allah. Muhammad is the Messenger of Allah."

2. Title given to a person who has completed the pilgrimage (Hajj) to Mecca.

3. These are the kinds of verses used to subjugate Christians and Jews living under Islamic law during the Middle Ages; see

discussion on dhimmis in chapter 13, Islamic Migration and Mission and the implementation of this verse in the histories outlined in *Myth of the Andalusian Paradise* by Dario Morera, pages 19–36.

4. See a summary of latest findings on pfanderfilms, YouTube, from a team who study ancient texts and history.

5. Georges Houssney, *Engaging Islam* (Lafayette, CO: Treeline Publishing, 2010) is excellent, especially for an American context. Nabeel Qureshi, *Seeking Allah, Finding Jesus* (Grand Rapids, MI: Zondervan, 2016) is an inspiring story of a Muslim becoming a Christian, filled with helpful Christian apologetics and insight into the love a Muslim family has of Islam.

6. A different view from this book can be found in Miroslav Volf's, *Allah: A Christian Response* (San Francisco: Harper One, 2012).

Chapter 8

1. These details in this section come from multiple sources. Any details of the founders of the schools of law are from Islamic tradition, not necessarily from history. Islamfiqh.net provides some insights into how Muslims consider Islamic law.

2. Saudi leaders "are active and diligent" using their considerable financial resources "in funding and promoting Salafism all around the world." Mark Durie, "Salafis and the Muslim Brotherhood: What Is the Difference?," Middle East Forum, June 6, 2013, https://www.meforum.org/3541/salafis-muslim-brotherhood.

3. They are the compilers of these Hadith according to Islamic traditions but not necessarily according to the latest research on its history.

4. Also written as Shi'ite, Shiite, Shia.

5. Shi'a means "follower."

6. Al-Islam.org is a Shi'a online resource, with downloadable books to help understand Shi'ah traditions and theology, , https://www.al-islam.org/islam-faith-practice-history-sayyid-muhammad-rizvi/lesson-17-twelve-caliphs-or-imams.

7. The imams are usually referred to by their first name and their title combined as in: Ali al-Murtaza. Sometimes the titles and spellings differ between Sunni and Shi'a sources, Arabic and Persian languages, and different Islamic commentators. https://www.al-islam.org/shiite-encyclopedia/twelve-imams-part-1.

8. Sharif Razi, *Nahjul Balagha Part 1, The Sermons*, accessed April 9, 2023, https://www.al-islam.org/nahjul-balagha-part-1-sermons.

9. Bernie Power, *Understanding Jesus and Muhammad: What the Ancient Texts Say about Them* (Sydney, Australia: Acorn Press, 2016), 32.

10. For more on the topic see Samuel Green, "The Gospel of Barnabas," accessed April 9, 2023, https://www.answering-islam.org/Green/barnabas.htm. Answering-Islam has a vast compilation of answers to Islamic polemics against Christianity.

Chapter 9

1. Bernie Power, *Understanding Jesus and Muhammad* (Alma, MI: Morning Star Publishing, 2015), 39–44, 45.

2. For succinct downloadable tables comparing Jesus, Isa, and Muhammad, see One Truth Project, accessed April 10, 2023, https://www.onetruthproject.org/resources.

3. Likely a reference to the bump seen on committed Muslim foreheads, because they pray five times a day, meaning their forehead hits their prayer carpet (or a stone if a Shi'a Muslim) five times a day.

4. A. Guillaume, translator, *The Life of Muhammad* (Oxford: Oxford University Press, 1982), and Rizwi Faizer, editor, *The Life of Muhammad, al-Waqidi's Kitab al-Maghazi* (Abingdon, England: Routledge, 2011).

5. Tom Holland's book, *In the Shadow of the Sword*, highlights scholarly work on Islam's origins, such as Patricia Crone, John Wansbrough, and Andrew Rippin, among others. *In the Shadow of the Sword: The Birth of Islam and the Rise of the Global Arab Empire* (Hachette, UK: Little, Brown and Company, 2012). Also see his excellent gentle film, *Islam: The Untold Story*.

6. One of the earliest Qur'anic manuscripts was found in Sana, Yemen. It has been dated to around AD 705. It is shorter than most Qur'ans with many suras not found within it and with theological differences to the Qur'ans used today.

7. For accessible and up-to-date discussions on the subject, see Jay Smith, "Engaging Islam, While Loving Muslims," discussing the latest research, accessed April 10, 2023, https://www.youtube.com/@pfanderfilms.

8. For a detailed read on the topic, though shocking in parts, see Dario Fernandez-Morera, *The Myth of the Andalusian Paradise: Muslims, Christians, and Jews under Islamic Rule in Medieval Spain* (Wilmington, DE: ISI Books, 2016).

Chapter 10

1. Current commentators tend to use the term *Islamist* or *extremist* to refer to Muslims who engage in terror activities. *Radical* implies a "rooted" belief, Muslims who are passionate about their religious texts, which is why we have used the term in this book.

2. Sayyid Qutb, *In the Shade of the Qur'an: Fi Zilal al-Qur'an*, vol. 1, translator Adil Salahi, (The Islamic Foundation; revised ed., 2003).

3. See an early biography of Muhammad's raids: Rizwi Faizer, *The Life of Muhammad: Al-Waqidi's Kitab al-Maghazi*, 86, 201–22, 383–84.

4. Dario Fernandez-Morera, *The Myth of the Andalusian: Muslims, Christians, and Jews under Islamic Rule in Medieval Spain* (Wilmington, DE: ISI Books, 2016).

5. Ed Husain, *The House of Islam: A Global History* (London: Bloomsbury Publishing, 2018).

6. Muhammad's child bride.

7. For a detailed study of the Hadith, see Bernie Power, *Challenging Islamic Traditions: Searching Questions about the Hadith from a Christin Perspective* (Pasadena: William Carey Library, 2016).

8. See Amina Wadud, *Qur'an and Woman: Rereading the Sacred Text from a Woman's Perspective* (Oxford: Oxford University Press, 1999), for a detailed discussion on Qur'anic interpretation from a modernist position.

9. Murtaza Mutahhari, *On the Islamic Hijab* (New York: International Publishing Company, 2002), 5. This opinion is especially evident among radical Muslims.

10. Widely distributed tracts on the topic written by Islamic scholars who misrepresent biblical teaching enable the proliferation of this belief. See, Dr. Jamal A. Badawi, *The Status of Women in Islam* (Birmingham: Islamic Propagation Centre International, no date given), 8, 20.

11. The information under the subtitle "Poles Apart" has been adapted from my thesis, "Women in Islam: Modern Arguments and Internal Debates," London School of Theology, 2007.

Chapter 11

1. Islamic texts are compilations of different books, as is the Bible. The Qur'an is also a compilation of books, though they can also be called chapters.

2. Mary Jo Sharpe, an assistant professor of apologetics at Houston Christian University, and I have both publicly debated a Muslim academic on the topic of women in Islam.

3. Burak Bekdil, *Erdogan: No Moderate Islam*, Middle East Forum, December 4, 2017, https://www.meforum.org/7078/erdogan-no-moderate-islam.

4. John Allembhillah Azumah, *The Legacy of Arab-Islam in Africa: A Quest for Inter-religious Dialogue* (Oneworld Academic, 2001).

5. Fraizer Rizwi, ed., *The Live of Muhammad, Al Waqidi's Kitab al-Maghazi* (Routledge: Oxfordshire, 2011), 199–202, 382–84.

6. For a brief introduction on these topics, see Beth Peltola and Tim Dieppe, *Questions to Ask Your Muslim Friends: A Closer Look at Islamic Beliefs and Texts* (London: Wilberforce Publications, 2022), chapter 6 on women.

7. Dario Fernandez-Morera, *The Myth of the Andalusian Paradise* (ISI Books, Wilmington, Delaware, 2016), 65, 205–33.

8. Fernandez-Morera, *The Myth of the Andalusian Paradise*, 206–7.

9. To further understand dhimmitude, see Mark Durie, *The Third Choice: Islam, Dhimmitude and Freedom* (Melbourne,

Australia: Deror Books, 2010); also see Bat Ye'or, *The Dhimmi: Jews and Christians under Islam* (Cranbury, NJ: Associated University Presses, 1985).

10. Ibn Hayyan (d. 1075), a Muslim historian, speaks of this in *Muqtabis V*, 322–23; referenced in Dario Fernandez-Morera, *The Myth of the Andalusian Paradise: Muslims, Christians, and Jews under Islamic Rule in Medieval Spain* (Wilmington, DE: ISI Books, 2016), 130.

Chapter 12

1. Examples include Dr. Timothy Winter, faculty of Divinity, at the University of Cambridge; Ed Hussain, author of *The House of Islam*, who states in his book his role in advising international governments; Mohammed Abdul Muqtedar Khan, professor of political sciences at the University of Delaware; and Hamza Yusuf, who began his Islamic life as a Sufi but now holds to mainstream Islamic views. Yusuf is the founder of the Zaytuna Institute in Berkeley, California, the first accredited Muslim college in America.

Chapter 13

1. Ibn Ishaq and Alfred Guillaume, *The Life of Muhammad: A Translation of Ibn Ishaq's Sirat Rasul Allah* (Oxford: Oxford University Free, 1955), 308, 337.

2. For more on the topic, see Sam Solomon, *Modern Day Trojan Horse: Al-Hijra, the Islamic Doctrine of Immigration, Accepting Freedom or Imposing Islam?* (Afton, VA: Advancing Native Missions, 2009).

3. Bat Ye'or, *Understanding Dhimmitude* (New York: RVP Press, 2013), 56–62. Also see Bat Ye'or, *Jews and Christians under Islam* (Madison, NJ: Fairleigh Dickinson University Press, 1985).

4. Bat Ye'or, *Jews and Christians under Islam* (Madison, NJ: Fairleigh Dickinson University Press, 1985).

5. Hanbali law. Shayk Salih ibn Fawzan al-Fawzan, *A Commentary on Zad al-Mustaqni: Imam al-Hajjawai's (d. 968 [AD 1561]) Classical Guide to the Hanbali Madhab* (Birmingham, UK: Dar al-Arqam Publishing, 2016), 770–71.

Chapter 14

1. Psalm 96 is a great starting point, as are Isaiah 41:10; Deuteronomy 31:6; Romans 1:16; and we can't forget Matthew 28:18–20.

Chapter 16

1. Michael Reeves, *The Good God: Enjoying Father, Son and Spirit* (Milton Keynes, UK: Paternoster, 2012); Lee Strobel, *In Defense of Jesus* (Grand Rapids, MI: Zondervan, 2016); Steve Cowan and Terry Wilder, eds., *In Defence of the Bible: A Comprehensive Apologetic for the Authority of Scripture* (Nashville: B&H Academic, 2013).

2. Muslim missionaries train fellow Muslims to refer to words like *beget* in this passage to have only one meaning. In this instance, *beget* to them means Jesus is biologically from the Father, so we sometimes have to point out to them the richness of language, and that words often have multiple meanings. In reference to Christ, *beget* means "given" by God.

Chapter 17

1. Samuel Zwemer has written an excellent book that is now out of print but still accessible online. It is worth exploring for further discussion and greater understanding. Samuel Zwemer, *The Moslem Doctrine of God* (New York: American Tract Society, 1905).

2. You will note that some of Allah's names are not directly mentioned in the Qur'an, rather they are gleaned from multiple and general Islamic statements. Names are sometimes different in English language lists of the ninety-nine names.

3. As rendered in the Pickthall translation.

4. This verse is an example of how Allah's names are gleaned from overall themes in the text. English language versions of the Qur'an may also use different words to the Arabic versions.

5. Paul Blackham's study guide and TV series on Exodus are especially helpful to work through with Muslim friends. As he debated with Muslim missionaries to the West, he began to look deeper into the Trinity and the Lord Jesus as seen through the Old and New Testaments. Paul Blackham, *Book by Book Study Guide: Exodus* (London: Biblical Frameworks, 2012), https://biblicalframeworks.com and @Paulblackham.

Chapter 18

1. Bedford hours, Pris, c. 1410–30, MS 18850, fol.113v, the Trinity with scenes of the day of creation, found in Lucy Freeman Sandler, *Penned and Painted: The Art and Meaning of Books in Medieval and Renaissance Manuscripts* (London: British Library, 2022), 46–47.

2. Bernie Power, whose Arabic classes have been incredibly helpful, has provided deep insights into the Arabic meaning of the Qur'an. See his book, *Engaging Islamic Traditions: Using the Hadith in Christian Ministry to Muslims* (Pasadena, CA: William Carey Library, 2016), 114.

3. Cited from my Arabic class with Bernie Power, February 2023.

4. As rendered in the Pickthall Quran translation.

Chapter 21

1. Defining what a Christian is for your Muslim neighbor might be needed, as "the West" or "Hollywood" is deemed "Christian" in the minds of many Muslims.

Chapter 22

1. Rizwi Faizer, ed., *The Life of Muhammad, Al-Waqidi's Kitb al-Maghazi* (Oxford: Routledge, 2011), 384.

2. Dario Fernandez-Morera, *The Myth of the Andalusian: Muslims, Christians, and Jews under Islamic Rule in Medieval Spain* (Wilmington, DE: ISI Books, 2016), 128–32.

3. Some long-held Islamic beliefs do not directly come out of the Qur'an. This is one example, which is gleaned from Islamic traditions and the Tafsir (Islamic commentaries on the Qur'an). Qur'an 36:65–66 implies a struggle for some on judgment day to find their way.

Conclusion

1. Islam as a religion may have started toward the end of the seventh century and early eighth century, sixty to one hundred years after Muhammad died. From an Islamic perspective it rose to power in the early to mid-seventh century. For ease we will go with this earlier date, keeping in mind that latest research is revealing a different scenario.

2. Apart from the fact that much of the known Islamic world today used to be Christian or pagan, details of the invasions, destruction of property and literature, and enslavement are detailed in Dario Fernandez-Morera, *The Myth of the Andalusian Paradise: Muslims, Christians, and Jews under Islamic Rule in Medieval Spain* (Wilmington, DE: ISI Books, 2016), 43, 129, 124, 402.

ALSO AVAILABLE
IN THIS SERIES

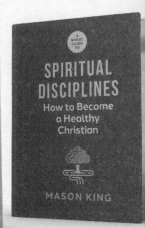